Supporting the prime and specific areas of development

What does it mean to be four?

What every practitioner needs to understa
about the development of four-year-old

Jennie Lindon

Updated in accordance with the 2012 Early Years Foundation Stage

Contents

Published by Practical Pre-School Books, A Division of MA Education Ltd,
St Jude's Church, Dulwich Road, Herne Hill, London, SE24 0PB.
Tel: 020 7738 5454
www.practicalpreschoolbooks.com
© MA Education Ltd 2012
All images © MA Education Ltd. Photos taken by Lucie Carlier and Ben Suri.

ISBN 978-1-907241-41-3

Focus on four-year-olds

What does it mean to be four? explores the developmental needs and likely skills of four-year-olds. The approach and ideas of this book are relevant to practitioners who are working with fours anywhere in the UK. However, the structure of the book follows the statutory framework for England of the Birth to Five Early Years Foundation Stage (EYFS). This new edition of *What does it mean to be four?* has been updated following the revised framework that came into force from September 2012. The main EYFS documents can be accessed through the Department for Education website (details on page 52).

A learning journey across early childhood

In England, early years practitioners have been working within the EYFS since September 2008. The revised statutory framework and supporting guidance are much reduced in length and some details, like the early learning goals for the end of the stage, have been changed. Of course, everyone has to become familiar with the revised framework. Yet, early years provision with established best practice will not need to make sweeping changes to their

approach to children and families. The crucial elements of best practice have not changed.

One focus of change is that the six areas of learning from the first EYFS framework have become seven areas, divided into three **prime** and four **specific** areas. This framework is one way of considering the breadth of children's learning. Children do not, of course, learn in separate compartments; their learning crosses all the boundaries. The overall aim of identifying particular areas of learning remains to ensure that early years practitioners do not overlook important areas of development.

The rationale for identifying three **prime** areas of learning is that secure early development rests upon:

● Communication and language

● Physical development

● Personal, social and emotional development.

These three areas are identified as, 'particularly crucial for igniting children's curiosity and enthusiasm for learning, and for building their capacity to learn, form relationships and thrive' (DfE, page 4, 2012). The order above is the one given in the EYFS framework. I have moved personal, social and emotional development (PSED) to the front of the list for all the books in the *What does it mean to be...?* series. In terms of child development, it makes more sense to start with the crucial underpinning of PSED.

There is a sound developmental basis for arguing that, without secure personal, social and emotional development, young children spend considerable energy striving for affirmation that they are accepted and loved for themselves. Concern has grown over the shaky communication skills of some young children, whose early experiences have not supported their development. Children's ability and motivation to be an active communicator opens the door for other aspects of their development.

Making physical development a prime area is also welcome, since this aspect of how young children learn has often been undervalued. Young children need to have easy opportunities to be physically active, encouraged by adult play partners who do not try to curb natural exuberance. There is good reason to be concerned about the well-being of fours whose limited opportunities for active play have already pushed them into sedentary habits.

The four **specific** areas are:

- Literacy

- Mathematics

- Understanding the world

- Expressive arts and design.

The guidance for early years practice is that the three prime areas should be uppermost in the minds of practitioners working with younger children. The age range has not been made specific, although the implication is that this strong focus applies to working with under-threes. The four specific areas are still of relevance for very young children, but need to be fully understood in their baby, toddler or two-year-version. Four-year-old learning in these specific areas evolves from developmentally appropriate earlier experiences for very young children.

Practitioners' attention needs now to be spread relatively evenly over all seven areas. However, you continue to be very alert to the prime areas, which remain the foundation for secure learning within the four specific areas. If fours are struggling with shaky confidence, an ability to express their thoughts in words or uncertain physical skills, then your main focus must be there. You need to identify the nature of the problem and how you can best help children, in partnership with their family.

'Early Education' (2012) was commissioned by the DfE to produce the supporting non-statutory guidance across the

Birth to Five age range. This document explains the four main themes of the EYFS: A Unique Child, Positive Relationships, Enabling Environments and how they contribute to the fourth theme, Learning and Development. The guidance also includes a revised version of 'Development Matters', cut back in line with the much reduced number of early learning goals (ELGs) for the end of the EYFS. This material offers ideas about how supportive practitioners behave with babies and children and what they could provide within the learning environment. These suggestions should refresh and inform best early years practice. They are not a have-to-do checklist.

The document provides some developmental highlights for children's journey towards the early learning goals. This resource continues with the previous EYFS approach of broad and overlapping age spans: birth to 11 months, 8-20 months, 16-26 months, 22-36 months, 30-50 months and 40-60+ months. The developmental information is a reminder of the kinds of changes likely to happen, if all is going well with babies and young children. They are, for instance, a brief reminder of the early part of the learning journey towards literacy or numeracy. The items are not an exhaustive list of everything that happens.

As with the first EYFS framework, these developmental highlights, and linked practical advice, were neither developed, nor intended to be used, as a checklist to assess children. Their value is dependent on the secure child development knowledge of practitioners using the resource.

The aim is to refresh about realistic expectations, supporting practitioners to focus on the uniqueness of individual babies and children and to protect time for them to enjoy secure learning over early childhood. Managers and practitioners all need to understand that none of the descriptions, with the sole exception of the ELGs, are required targets to be observed or assessed.

Child-focused observation and assessment

The revised EYFS continues to highlight the importance of ongoing observation, which enables practitioners to shape learning experiences that are well attuned to the interests and abilities of individual babies and young children. The revised statutory framework stresses that much of this observation arises within day-by-day alert looking and listening. Some practitioners call this informal or incidental observation and sometimes, not always, it may be captured with a brief written note or a photo.

All children should have a reliable and descriptive personal record, which will include some more organised observations. The revised EYFS gives very clear direction that the process of observation and assessment, *'should not entail prolonged breaks from interaction with children, nor require excessive paperwork. Paperwork should be limited to that which is absolutely necessary to promote children's successful learning and development'* (DfE, page 10, 2012).

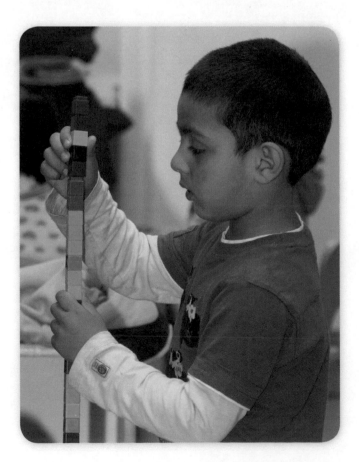

The situation continues to be that, except for the EYFS profile, there are no statutory written formats for observation and assessment, nor for any kind of flexible forward planning. Early years settings and childminders can continue to use approaches that have worked well so far. The only difference is that layouts will need to be changed in line with the seven areas of development. Established best early years practice is not challenged by the revised EYFS framework.

Attentive and knowledgeable key persons will continue to be aware, and keep some records, of the progress of individual children over time. Observant practitioners will learn from watching, listening and being a play partner to children. These observations, often acted upon but not written down, will make a difference to the detail of what is offered to individuals and to sensible short-term changes in planned opportunities for a group of children. Flexible, forward planning will continue to be responsive to the needs and interests of individual babies and children: through continuous provision (the learning environment) and flexible use of planned activities.

The revised EYFS has introduced a new element to the statutory requirements for early years provision. From September 2012 there must be a descriptive individual assessment within the year that children are two: a two-year-old progress check focused especially on the three prime areas of development. All early years provision with two-year-olds must organise this developmental assessment, by the key person. This check is described in detail in *What does it mean to be two?* (2012). For practitioners who work with four-year-olds, this progress check will be part of the existing record for individual children.

The revised EYFS still applies to the end of the reception year, at which point children are assessed through a revised and much shorter EYFS Profile. The meaningless numerical scoring system has also disappeared. The total number of early learning goals (ELGs) has been significantly reduced from 69 to 17, and with some different wording. All the ELGs apply to the end of the phase of early childhood: specifically to the level of progress expected by the end of the summer term of the academic year in which a child reaches five years of age. At this point some children will be well through their personal twelve months of being five. However, summer born children will still be very young fives and 'summer holiday' born children are still waiting for their fifth birthday.

Sound knowledge of child development

Practitioners' existing knowledge can be supplemented by the 'Development Matters' guidance materials mentioned on page 3. These developmental highlights are intended to remind and provoke further ideas about what you may have noticed. This resource can operate as a support, but will not substitute for a thorough knowledge of child development, gained within initial training and refreshed as part of continued professional development.

In terms of the overlapping age bands, practitioners working with four-year-olds will mainly look at the 40-60+ months span. However, if you are responsible for fours, whose experience so far has been very unfavourable, then you may need to look at the 30-50 months band, at least for some areas of learning. This younger age band might also be more relevant for disabled four-year-olds. It depends on the nature and severity of the disability; the key person will have to use professional judgement.

If disability is an issue, then it is likely that the family of a four-year-old will have a diagnosis and be able to share with you how the disability or chronic health condition affects their child. However, circumstances vary and you may support a family through the realisation that their child's unusual pattern of development, perhaps for communication or physical skills, is not 'just a phase' that will pass.

Usual good practice for partnership applies: you talk with parents to understand their child as an individual with familiar routines, likes and dislikes. Parents will be able to tell you, as a childminder or the child's key person in nursery, about their child's current ability level and any special help that will be needed. You are not expected to know everything about every disability. Good practice is to know how to find out more. Parents will be experts about their own child but may not necessarily have had much help so far, especially if their young child's disability was not apparent until recently. In a group setting, the SENCO should have more specialised knowledge and local contacts.

Ready for school?

Practitioners in England working with four-year-olds, especially the older fours (and if you work in a reception class), will be alert to the ELGs. Responsible and knowledgeable practitioners are very aware of the learning environment and supportive relationships that fours need, if their development is to progress securely. Young children deserve to be protected from an intellectual rat race. They have the right to enjoy their personal learning journey, and not be harassed into a premature dash towards the ELGs for the end of this stage.

The revised EYFS statutory framework talks of ensuring, children's 'school readiness' (DfE, page 2, 2012) and ensuring that 'they are ready for school' (DfE, page 4, 2012). There are good reasons to be wary about what these phrases mean in practice. Official pronouncements from the previous Labour government, as well as the Coalition government (of the time of writing in 2012), have focused more on delivering children as classroom-ready. The previous and current governments have shown a disturbing tendency to talk about reception class as if

it is the beginning of statutory education in England – which it is not. Best practice for any kind of transition – and this move is an important one for young children – is to focus on the readiness of the next stage (Year 1) to welcome fives as they are.

Developmentally appropriate practice is the same as responsible adult behaviour: both focus on realistic expectations of what fours, and then fives, are likely to be able to manage. Practice and related adult actions focus clearly on avoiding any demands that are very likely to undermine children's confidence and positive disposition to learn. A continuing problem with the revised EYFS is that the early learning goals for literacy are still unrealistic for five-year-olds, especially since only a minority of the group will be rising sixes in the summer term of reception class.

It is also crucial that practitioners and parents do not panic, thinking that most children, with ordinary support, will somehow not be 'ready for school'. Some official comments have implied that there is a serious problem of 'unreadiness' in the youngest generation. The revised EYFS has a positive focus on early intervention, which is necessary for children from vulnerable families. However, the reality is that most young children, and their families, are doing fine. Young children must not treated as if the whole group has serious problems; most of them do not need focused intervention. Children will continue doing well with best early years practice and committed early years practitioners – so long as Year 1, and not reception class, is seen properly as the transition year into the more formal classroom model.

Four-year-olds will benefit from a developmentally appropriate perception of support towards the transition into primary school. Practitioners and parents need to consider what helps children, including what will cause them difficulties, if familiar adults overlook vital skills and dispositions. From the perspective of young girls and boys, what most helps them is that they have been enabled to:

● Develop a positive disposition to learning: enthusiasm, a can-do outlook with a robust view that mistakes are not disasters.

● Behave as independent learners within a familiar context: confident to ask for guidance, when they need it, believing that adults should help you.

● Become competent in most of their self-care, with more support for children who live with a disability or chronic health condition.

● Become confident in holding a conversation, expressing opinions and steadily being able to manage the waiting that is involved in a small group discussion.

These points are discussed within this book. A child-friendly interpretation of the transition into primary school arises across all seven learning areas of the EYFS.

Personal, social and emotional development

You can see now the results of children's past experiences – family and early years provision – and secure foundations from sustained, affectionate relationships. Fours are alert observers; practitioners (and parents too) need to act as positive role models through what they say and do. All the early learning goals in PSED benefit from adult reflection along the lines of, 'Can the children see me behaving in this way? Am I setting a good example?'.

A positive sense of 'self'

Four-year-olds have developed a sense of self, based on their immediate family and social circle. Their explorations of 'what makes me, me' give rise to some of their searching questions and some of this intellectual exploration happens within the family. Fours are curious by nature and, if all has gone normal and well in their development, are well able to put their thoughts into words. Familiar adults in children's early years provision

will be asked similar questions, often provoked when fours recognise that the family life of their peers differs from their own.

Children can also have a sense of their own and family identity that extends into their local community and the people and places that they know. Their identity is grounded in their own family and friends network. However, this experience may support the very beginnings of understanding different social and cultural groups. This aspect of four-year-old knowledge has sometimes been over-estimated, especially when practitioners have been directed to run activities that are disconnected from first-hand experiences and children's existing knowledge base. Young children have to 'start with me' and extend into other familiar people and groups. Your aim is that individual children build a positive sense of themselves, that does not depend on being rude or dismissive about anyone else. This approach applies to all children and families, whether they would be classified as a minority group, or not.

Children can be building a positive view of themselves, which is nevertheless realistic. They need this secure foundation to be confident learners. Fours, who have experienced friendly guidance in the past, may feel disappointed, even sad, when a chosen project goes awry. However, there is a good chance that they will take a breath and set about finding out how to resolve the problem, rather than believe that mistakes are evidence that there is something the matter with them. In contrast, the reactions of some fours will alert their key person to a child's fragile sense of self-esteem.

Young children vary, of course, in how swiftly they feel able to bounce back from difficulties. They show their individual temperament, as well as the unique pattern of their experience. Yet, some fours appear to be very uncertain of their own worth; events so far have not enabled them to build a secure emotional base. Perhaps they are very concerned to get everything exactly 'right' or have already become convinced, from harsh adult criticism, that they 'cannot' do something or are 'useless'. These young boys and girls will need careful support, if they are to build their self-confidence. If the source of undermining comes from home, the key person will also seek to communicate positive ways of helping children learn, rather than focusing exclusively on what has gone wrong.

Four-year-olds are more able than younger children to manage the social interaction that goes on in a group of children supported by an adult, but they still need to feel they are getting personal attention. Fours are not ready for the more formal approach of the school classroom: a particular type of large group situation and a specialised learning environment. Fours are able to cope with conversational small group interaction, but a classroom approach requires patterns of behaviour that are unrealistic to expect of fours (Lindon, 2012). Their transition towards primary school should be a steady process, not a harassed and premature rush.

The journey towards emotional literacy

Four-year-olds have made progress in learning about their own emotions and have some understanding that other people, adults as well as children, also have feelings. Some four-year-olds are able to express their feelings in words as well as the body language that communicates happiness,

---

WHAT ARE CHILDREN LEARNING?

You cannot directly observe a child's sense of personal identity. You can, however, make well-supported guesses from what young boys and girls say out loud and the questions they want to ask you.

You can read an example from one four-year-old on this page. This description is a reminder of how children's learning crosses the boundaries of the different areas of learning. This example could have been placed with Communication and Language or with Understanding the world.

Of course, individual fours will each ask a different sequence of questions. What have you noticed from the four-year-olds you know well? How are they trying to make sense of their personal world and their place in it? When fours talk about their family it is very likely that you will have to ask questions in your turn, so that you can understand who is 'Pops'.

See what else comes up in conversation with parents. If necessary, reassure them about the importance of giving time and attention to such questions, even if they come at an inconvenient time to the adults.

LOOKING CLOSELY AT FOURS

As a very young four, my son Drew was keen to work out family relationships. He returned to this subject, like other topics that interested him, several times over a matter of weeks. He asked direct questions, but also checked his understanding by comments made with a questioning tone in his voice.

Drew worked out that he was older than his sister, Tanith, because he was born first. He then explored the business of being older and being a brother or sister. Drew worked out that you did not have to be older to be a brother. He needed to check this fact because the other family he knew best was also a boy followed by a younger sister. Drew grasped the logic that he was a brother because he was a boy; that was the key point, not being the older one.

Drew also discovered steadily by his questions that familiar people had different roles in our family network. He was intrigued that I was 'Mummy' to him and Tanith, but also 'daughter' to his grandmother Nangi and 'sister' to my own brother. Grandma was Daddy's Mummy and – surprising for Drew to discover – Daddy had once been small. So maybe one day Drew would be as big as Daddy.

Halfway through the year that he was four, Drew met the part of our family based in the United States. He set off once again to explore how everyone linked together. He developed almost a quiz style, asking: "Who is Mummy's Mummy?" and "who is Tracy's (his cousin) Daddy's Daddy?".

---

excitement, distress or frustration. These children have an emotional vocabulary, gained from experience of real situations in which familiar adults have used words appropriate to describing what was happening. This adult thoughtfulness needs to be applied for all children; boys are as able as girls to use an emotional vocabulary when they have been part of such conversations. These conversations are genuine reactions to actual events; they are not pre-planned, adult-led group discussions about emotions in the abstract.

Young children start with awareness of their own feelings – again 'starting with me' – and become steadily able to consider the likely feelings of other people. Fours, who are confident about respect from adults about what they feel, are far more likely to voice their good guesses about how another child might feel. Children do not immediately leap to understanding the emotions of other people. They need the firm foundation of knowing what happy, sad or disappointed feel like inside for them. Children may show their insights by comments that show their understanding of how another child might be upset.

Children need the words for a wide range of emotions: 'thrilled', 'curious' or 'puzzled' are just as important as 'cross' or 'hurt'. Yet, it is true that feelings like anger and frustration can emerge in strong words and actions that disrupt the peace of a nursery or childminder's home. In a supportive emotional environment some four-year-olds are able to link events with feelings, such as: "I'm cross with him because he knocked my tower down!". With support they are able to use their words, rather than a physical expression of just how cross they currently feel.

Young children do not think in abstractions about 'being nice' or 'thinking of other people's feelings' without any context. Four-year-olds relate such ideas to real people and places. They have experience they can draw upon of: "When people are nice or nasty to me" and increasingly that "it's nice to make sure my friend has enough bricks" or "it's horrible if you hurt yourself and nobody cares". They can step beyond their own experience, but four-year-olds need to be able to connect ideas or else they are just so many words.

Social skills of four-year-olds

Close friendships can develop between four-year-olds, whose early years provision is organised in ways that enable and encourage social contact. Nursery heads and childminders need to ensure that flexibility for adults in terms of a child's

LOOKING CLOSELY AT FOURS

In New River Green Centre, a conversation unfolded between a practitioner (Ria) and more than one child (threes as well as fours). The children wanted to express concern that a young boy had Megan's special handbag that she had brought in today. Their non-verbal behaviour was of worry for a precious item; there was no undertone of 'telling on' another child.

Ria took what the children said with seriousness and reassured them with: "He's her brother. That's alright, she's allowed him to have her bag". Megan, who was close by, confirmed that the younger child was her brother and that she had given his permission. A lot of reassuring nodding went on.

There was a short pause and then another child noticed that the same younger brother was wearing only his socks with: "He hasn't got his shoes on". Ria thanked the child who spoke and said to the younger boy: "You need your shoes". The boy (2 years) cooperatively got off his bike, went up to outdoor shelf full of Wellington boots and found his pair. He put them on and returned to his bike.

Ria was responding to naturally occurring events. Consider what messages her behaviour gave to the children, especially those who had felt confident to voice their concerns about the well-being of other children.

PARTNERSHIP WITH PARENTS: TALKING ABOUT FEELINGS AND ACTIONS

The development of children's emotional literacy is dependent upon emotionally literate behaviour from their familiar adults. Early years practitioners and parents need to be comfortable to talk about feelings, as this opportunity arises, within the normal to-and-fro of a day with children.

You look for opportunities to share wise adult behaviour with parents. Adults definitely do not talk at length about feelings – you would soon lose children's interest and attention. Your comments are brief and to the point: "You look very pleased with your tower" and "you've got your sad face on – what's happened?".

You speak with children at the time. You do not save up comments for later. Later in the day, four-year-olds may well remember the event that you now want to discuss with them. However, they will very likely be puzzled over the point of talking now: the moment has long passed.

LOOKING CLOSELY AT FOURS

In Mary Paterson Nursery School, Jasmine (4yrs, 5mths) engaged me in conversation about a picture taped to the piano. She commented: "That's a scary lady" and invited me to look very closely. I suggested that maybe the lady's expression was 'serious', because she was concentrating on her painting. Jasmine looked doubtful and I asked: "What makes you say she's scary?" Jasmine did an accurate imitation of the lady's face, as if to indicate that was evidence enough. I said: "Fair enough, you feel she looks scary".

Jasmine suggested the picture could go in the bin. I proposed that maybe she should ask the others, because everyone might not find this lady scary. We chatted a bit about what else Jasmine could do: not look at the picture/fold it up/make faces back.

attendance does not become unpredictability for young children. Some firm friendships are established between boys and girls, although fours play quite a lot with children of their own sex. Of course, friends can and do fall out sometimes. However, relaxed social contact within play offers many opportunities for four-year-olds to learn that their peers have a different viewpoint and that differences do not have to be a problem.

Social relations within play are sophisticated and adults are responsible for making sure they understand the situation, rather than assuming one child or a small group is being unpleasant. Sometimes playing children have done their level best to accommodate a less easy play companion. They have now finally had enough of a peer who disrupts the game with messing about or bossiness. Fours also become irritated with peers who burst into tears at minor setbacks or if they cannot get their own way.

Early years practitioners should be observant to ensure that children do not reject each other solely on the basis of their sex, ethnic group or disability. However, you should not assume that problems in play must be explained by rejection on the basis of group identity, simply because the children differ in this way. In a friendly atmosphere where adults discreetly oil the social wheels, young children build friendships across any 'boundaries' of grouping: age, social, ethnic or religious groups, language differences and across disability. However, children find it hard to sustain friendly relations when they cannot find shared ground, or if this other child struggles to be a friendly play partner.

Responsible early years practitioners look for how best to help with social problems in play. Fours can be very inventive to get around different home languages in a group. However, the

continued lack of a shared language may complicate play that depends on spoken communication, such as the imaginative role play scenarios that are played out by many fours. Children whose disabilities make it hard for them to understand the subtleties of play– for instance, children with autistic spectrum disorder – may not be easy play companions. Childminders and the key person in nursery have to look for careful and structured help for the child who is perplexed by aspects of social life with peers. Practitioners need to hold fair and realistic expectations of other four-year-olds, who will have limits to their tolerance for disruption to play.

So long as they have had social experiences in earlier childhood, four-year-olds have some strategies for approaching an existing group of playing children. They may ask to join them, edge in by playing alongside or perhaps make a suggestion. Again, so long as fours have had an environment in which to hone their social skills of play, girls and boys are able to initiate or follow in a small friendship group or pairs of children. Four-year-olds, who are at ease with each other, often develop long sequences in which the lead passes between individuals in a small group of children. This level of skill is less likely to have developed if children's play has been over-organised by adults – practitioners or parents.

Four-year-olds who have had supportive adults can be adept in many familiar social situations. However, they appreciate adult

help when a situation has become too complex or emotionally heated for them to resolve. Sometimes the problem is that children do not want to play with a peer who really wants to play with them, or continue with a game that the first child regards as finished. Fours, like fives and any children, want adults to come alongside and help to resolve a situation. They do not usually want adults to zoom in and take over; the exception is when something genuinely scary has happened.

Four-year-olds can learn and use the problem solving skills of conflict resolution, so long as familiar adults understand and support that development (Evans, 2002). You focus on acknowledging children's feelings and helping them to tell you 'what has happened?'. The message is 'what's the problem here?' rather than 'whose fault is it?'.

Sometimes, four-year-olds accept the perspective that 'it was an accident' or say on their own behalf: "I didn't mean to spill the water". In a warm emotional environment, such comments can be followed by a spontaneous and genuine, "I'm sorry about your painting". However, fours are keen observers and have sharp memories for unfairness and a repeating pattern. Children will sometimes make the judgement of 'but, he keeps crashing into me. He must be more careful' or that an adult should now stop a younger child who 'keeps messing up our game!'.

Four-year-olds do not grasp abstract 'whys' that are unconnected with events and relationships they understand. Nor do four or

five-year-olds need to be able to voice complex reasons in order to demonstrate that they have developed a level of pro-social behaviour. There is not always a neat match between what four-year-olds may be able to say is the 'right' thing to do and actually doing it. There are many reasons why it can be very hard to do the right thing, if you are four years old. It is also sobering to recall that there is usually an imperfect match between what grown ups say they would do, if faced by a imaginary scenario, and what they actually do in the real-life situation.

Four-year-olds steadily learn to make considerate choices in their own behaviour. They need familiar adults who set a good example and are fully aware of their own choices in behaviour. Genuinely helpful adults tune-in to four-year-old thinking and respect the boundaries to what young children can manage. They certainly avoid expectations of consistently 'good' behaviour that would most likely not be met by adults, let alone young children.

Simple rules, expressed as a positive 'do', and with an obvious link to context, make sense to four-year-olds. The exception will be children whose familiar adults have not set fair boundaries or who have been inconsistent and unpredictable. The underlying reasons, the 'why', need to be expressed in straightforward and practical terms. Children understand logic like, 'we put the toys back where they belong, because then we can all find them again' or 'you don't say that word because it is unkind and words can hurt you inside'.

The importance of nurture

Four-year-olds are still young children. We may be tempted to think of them as the 'older' ones, but this word only comes to mind because there are much younger children within the span of early childhood. On the other hand, fours are definitely not 'still babies' and it does them no favours to under-estimate their ability and self-awareness. They have developed from their three-year-old selves and, so long as they have had the adult support they deserve, young boys and girls can be very competent.

Fours still need to feel emotionally safe and at ease with their familiar and important adults – in early years provision just as in their own family home. Many of this age group still need the reassurance of a special toy or cuddly. Fours still need a reassuring cuddle from time to time, but their need for friendly touch and close physical contact is not restricted to times of uncertainty or distress. Fours often want to say 'hello, I'm back!' with a full body hug or the cuddle that says 'haven't we done brilliantly!'. They want to get your attention by touch and accept that you do that as well.

Growing competence in self-care remains important for four-year-olds. Children feel more positive about themselves when they are able to undertake many of the tasks of dressing, eating and toileting. They also need to feel confident that respectful adult help is available when they need assistance. So long as they have been given time to learn when they were younger, fours are now able to deal with most of their undressing, dressing, simple personal hygiene, going to the toilet and organising themselves at mealtimes. They may struggle with the more fiddly clothes fastening or cutting up some food. It is also not unusual that, for top-notch hygiene, young fours may still need some help or guidance with wiping their bottom.

Sometimes competent four-year-olds just need a helping hand or feel like being cosseted a bit today. We are not so different ourselves as adults. This situation is different from fours whose previous experience has encouraged them to take a helpless outlook and wait until an adult does up their buttons or hangs up their outdoor coat. Fours' skills are likely to become less secure when children are required to apply them in a rush. Adults are responsible for resolving problems that arise from poor time management within the day and routines that end up being rushed.

LOOKING CLOSELY AT FOURS

In New River Green, the team (like other high quality settings) have established routines for mealtimes that respect the importance of this time of the day. I joined the three- and four-year-olds for lunch and they had lunch on tables that seated up to eight. One of these was known by the children as 'the sensible table', because it did not have an adult sitting there. Individual children were chosen each day as able to be trusted.

Teresa (the practitioner) was close by on the second table with other children. However, there was no sense whatsoever that you were not sensible if children sat with an adult; everyone got a chance to sit at the children-only table. Individual girls and boys sounded proud as they came across from washing their hands and announced: "I'm on the sensible table today".

All the children (3-, 4- and a few 5-year-olds because it was summer holiday time) dished up for themselves from open dishes. They all waited until everyone had served what they wanted. The two table groups were patient and they amused themselves by choosing to count how many children were here today (see page 33).

Someone asked from time to time: "Can we start now?" but accepted Teresa's explanation of: "Not yet, everybody hasn't got their food". One child per table took the beakers with drink around to everyone and set them on the table. The two children took great care and there was a relaxed feel to the mealtime.

LOOKING CLOSELY AT FOURS

Four-year-olds are usually well toilet trained, but there will be some times when children inadvertently wet themselves. It matters a very great deal how these accidents are handled by adults. A sensitive approach can help a child to feel better; and unkind approach can make a child feel foolish and mucky. Individual children vary a great deal, as I observed during my visit to St Peter's nursery class.

One girl was distressed at her accident and was immediately comforted by the practitioner who was with her outdoors. Nobody was even slightly cross. The child calmed and went to change her clothes accompanied by another practitioner. A short while later, the girl became upset once more and this second team member was just as supportive, halted in her help with changing and focused on the child, to reassure that nobody was cross, that these things happened.

A second child was positively chirpy about her accident. I was sitting close by and she told me: "I've wet myself a bit". She confidently sorted out dry clothes from the chest of drawers that children could access themselves. She put her damp clothes in the hanging bag for washing. This girl took her time and nobody asked her to hurry up. At one point in mid-change, she joined a group briefly and then had a chat with a practitioner to explain that she could not find a pair of trousers, but thought these leggings would suit. The adult agreed with her.

Communication and language

Even young fours come across as confident individuals, ready to speak up within their familiar small community. Girls and boys have opinions to express and questions to ask. Sometimes they clearly show awareness of the needs of other children, sometimes even of adults. However, these chatty, social children have not sprung into existence as a consequence of passing their fourth birthday.

Communicative four-year-olds

With appropriate experiences from earlier childhood, four-year-olds should now be confident in their skills of spoken communication. Some children will be confident in more than one language, although possibly more at ease in their most familiar language. There has been increasing concern about the communication skills of some young children. Exploration of delays or unusual patterns of development may reveal the impact of undiagnosed hearing loss (or intermittent loss), learning disabilities that affect the development of communication and specific language disorders.

However, some fours with limited skills of oral communication do not live with a disability. Their potential ability has been blocked by very limited experience of friendly communication with familiar adults: the main source of learning for babies and young children. Children learn to talk, to listen and to enjoy the give-and-take of spontaneous conversation as the result of many relaxed, personal exchanges with communicative grown-ups. Children do not learn to talk from hours of watching television or DVDs or playing with battery operated toys that 'talk' at them. Nor do they learn to communicate freely from very structured, adult-led communication in groups.

By now four-year-olds should have a substantial vocabulary. It should be a significant project to note down all the words that an individual child uses and understands, and a decent sample of their spontaneous phrases and sentences. Many four-year-olds often develop personal interests, pursued through information books, self-chosen play and the interest sparked by some television programmes. You would not expect four-year-olds to have exactly the same vocabulary. Young boys and girls extend their impressive store of words as a reflection of their interest in monster trucks, dinosaurs or tigers. I have certainly been given friendly lectures by four-year-olds who knew more than I did about sharks or racing cars. My education was extended by being shown pictures in a book about sharks, or having the cars lined up so that the different features could be identified.

Fours should have got to the point where they recognise words they do not yet know and ask: "What did you say?" or "what does that word mean?". Some children notice fine differences and may want to know "why do you call that a mug? It's a cup". Such conversations sometimes happen between a child and familiar adult. However, I have also observed similar exchanges, occasionally heated, between children; it matters a great deal to distinguish between types of footwear or that a coach is not the same as a bus. What do such examples tell you about the invisible thinking going on in four-year-old heads?

LOOKING CLOSELY AT FOURS

In New River Green, Megan (4 years) had brought in a personal item, her handbag. She wanted to show the contents of her handbag to Ria (a practitioner) who expressed genuine interest and followed Megan's lead. Something family-related in the handbag led to a question from Ria about Megan's family: "I thought you just had one brother?". Megan went on to explain in detail the members of her family and Ria listened carefully, reflecting back some of what Megan volunteered.

A short while later Megan was talking with another practitioner, Neela, about her journey to nursery this morning. Megan said proudly: "I crossed the road myself. I looked both ways". Neela asked: "Was Mummy beside you?" and Megan was firm that "I did it myself". She talked in some detail about how she knew how to cross the road and Neela listened, following Megan's lead. Megan also chatted about how she could find her way to nursery and announced: "I have a map", which she pulled out of her handbag.

Slightly later, Neela checked discreetly with Megan's mother, who had brought her to nursery. It was clear that Megan was keen to check the road herself and make decisions about crossing, but she had not been left alone to do so.

Young boys and girls use their words to express thoughts, plans and possibilities in their play or involvement in meaningful routines. Four-year-olds want to speak their interesting thoughts out loud and, with some individual variation, find it hard to wait for long before speaking. Young children do not tolerate the long waiting times imposed by large group, adult-led discussion. Fours can become more able to wait a little bit in a small group, when experience has told them that waiting does not mean being forgotten by the adult.

An intriguing development with fours is that they can show a wide use of language and this understanding will have been observable with older threes. Fours behave in ways that show they regard language as a 'tool' at their disposal. If you listen and note (mentally or actually keep a record), you will become aware that four-year-olds use spoken language with a range of different purposes. You encourage by having a broad use of language yourself, and a large vocabulary that you use in spontaneous conversation with the children.

Children use their words to tell and describe what is happening in front of them. However, they can also recount something that has happened from the recent past, with an understanding that this event has gone. They sometimes use this skill by inviting you to reminisce with 'do you remember when…?'. They are able to pose questions, sometimes tough ones that make you think. They often use a questioning tone with comments that flags up to an attentive adult that this child's underlying message is, 'have I got this right?' or 'is this how it works?'.

WHAT ARE CHILDREN LEARNING?

Older children often enjoy communicating with babies and toddlers. Fours gain pleasure from making younger ones laugh and are often very good at the repetitive 'do it again and again' games that under-twos adore. Such scenes are heart-warming as you watch, but it is worth reflecting on what else your informal observation tells you about this four-year-old's development. What kind of thinking power is needed to tune-in to a much younger child? What can you reasonably guess about their broader knowledge of the world?

Boys as well as girls show an impressive understanding of differences in communication, when they adjust their style of communication for babies or young toddlers. Four-year-olds who have contact with much younger children show an understanding that simpler words and sentence construction is necessary. In nurseries, childminders' homes and children's own family, four-year-olds often chose to 'read' a book to a younger child or to establish shared games that enable the younger child to have a clear role.

Four-year-olds are able to request that you or another child do something they wish or help them in some way. Fours vary a great deal but, with a polite adult model to imitate, they have often learned basic courtesies in words and body language to avoid blunt demands. Four-year-olds are often adept at using language to explain, justify or argue. Adults need to admire the use of language, even if four-year-old negotiation skills may still be a little raw around the edges. Sometimes an important adult role is to get across to intense four-year-olds that it is possible to hold different opinions on something important and still be friends.

Young children use their conversational skills within any welcoming situation. I have visited many settings in which lunch or snack times are genuinely social. This important routine of nurture has been given enough time, so it is perfectly possible to eat, drink and enjoy a good chat. The description on this page is just one example of excellent practice I have been able to observe.

Four-year-olds have a good grasp of basic grammar. However, they are still likely to make some logical mistakes, about generalising a regular grammatical rule to constructions that do not obey the usual pattern. They have usually grasped the power of the negative, along with the appropriate tone of voice, for instance with, 'It wasn't me!' or 'I didn't tear the book!'. They are able to use their words, with the appropriate tone of voice and emphasis to question and challenge, to tell and explain.

Some four-year-olds are already successfully bilingual. Some encounter a language different from their family home when they enter nursery or reception class. Around the world, not only in the UK, many children have more than one language. It is only monolingual adult speakers who think bilingualism has to be problematic. In diverse neighbourhoods and settings, monolingual four-year-olds can understand that not everyone speaks the same language, even that some kinds of writing look very different from each other. Children are often interested in languages other than their own that they can link with real people.

However, it is inaccurate to assume that children just 'pick up' a language in addition to their home language with no effort.

LOOKING CLOSELY AT FOURS

In Mary Paterson Nursery School, the entire routine of lunchtime is a relaxed, purposeful time. Some practitioners always sit and eat with the children, including the head. During my visits I listened to sustained conversations about what people had done that morning, but also events in a child's family, started by an adult's comment of "your mum told me you had a guest in your house".

Children sometimes like to discuss their meal. Fergus (4yrs, 7mths) had asked for 'sponge' and Caroline (the practitioner) explained that today's pudding was called a crumble. Fergus then asked for clarity: "What is sponge?" and Caroline explained the difference between sponge and crumble. Children also wanted to chat about food in general, for instance, one child wanted to know: "Why are peas good for you?". Several children lingered over their watermelon, because they were interested in all the seeds and what they were.

On one table the children themselves started a conversation about 'why you don't hit people back'. The adult listened and contributed the reminder that in the nursery it was understood that you put your hand up (in the stop sign) and say: "Stop. I don't like it. Don't hurt me". She confirmed that children can tell another child 'stop' themselves; they do not have to go and tell another adult. During my visits I observed two occasions when children felt at ease to do just that and were able to resolve a minor altercation in play.

Towards the end of one lunchtime, one boy was busy clearing up aprons and he had an armful. He stopped to have a chat with an adult at one table, telling her about how they make films in his family. A short conversation followed about what kind of films and whether the family then watched them on their television.

Children whose fluent language is not spoken in nursery, or not by many people, need support as they link up the words to familiar objects and experiences. Four-year-olds are often already aware of elements of the written form of their home language. Some children will encounter a different written script with their exposure to English.

Young children need to build a large working vocabulary and it is important not to underestimate this task for bilingual children. The revised EYFS has emphasised that proper respect for young children's home language(s) has to work alongside the responsibility of ensuring that they are gaining fluency in English: the shared language of the UK. The revised welfare requirements also emphasise it is vital that early years practitioners are all confident English speakers (DfE, page 17, 2012). This paragraph is an inclusive statement about the workforce, not applying specifically to bilingual practitioners.

The give-and-take of conversation

Four-year-olds do not need structured language programmes, unless their skills for communication are delayed or developmentally awry. Language is social and needs to be grounded in a meaningful context for talk. Babies and toddlers learn to talk by happy experiences of being talked with, long before they are contributing recognisable words. Fours continue their development with plenty of opportunities for chatting with familiar adults and also now with friends of a similar age.

Young children flourish in an environment where they can relax, have smaller indoor and outdoor spaces where is it comfortable to chat and a timing to their days which is respectful of conversational exchange. The give and take of normal conversation can unfold through shared activities and events, in which children and adults are engaged and enthused, dealing with practical problems to solve, memories to recall and share and the expression of ideas and opinions.

Four-year-olds are capable of the social skills needed for a conversation, so long as their experience has supported their learning. Conversational skills include not only talking, but also pausing to listen, linking what you say to what the other person has just said and being patient to wait your turn. Children learn from adult models, from having people show an interest in what they want to say and being given time to express themselves.

Children's use of language, their comments and questions are a valuable window onto their ways of thinking. Four-year-olds show you their expectations, interests and ways of thinking also through their behaviour, including play. But their spoken words, in conversation, with you or that you overhear between children, tell you volumes about what matters to these four-year-olds. In contrast, they are

unlikely to develop or show their conversational skills, if they experience a very structured day, with adults who determine a great deal of what happens, including what is judged to be worth talking about in adult-led exchanges.

Collecting children's questions is a worthwhile 'project'. If you realise that the fours in your provision do not ask you many questions, then it is definitely time to reflect on what is happening. Do some boys and girls need more experience to know that you are genuinely interested and happy for them to take time to organise their thoughts? You will not be impatient or interrupt, as perhaps they have experienced with other adults in the past. On the other hand, do you, or your colleagues, need to adjust your communication style? Perhaps you have established the expectation that you ask the questions and children give the answers.

Fours can be keen to drive their own learning and their chosen questions are at the cutting edge of what they currently know, and suspect they do not quite understand. Barbara Tizard and Martin Hughes (2002) made the very useful distinction that children's thinking develops along two equally important tracks:

● Children need to learn details and they are hungry for information. Children whose enquiries meet with a positive adult response go on to ask other questions when they are ready.

- But four-year-olds are also working hard on the context of knowledge that enables them to make sense of the information. Their questions sometimes show an awareness that something does not fit, a sense of 'but that can't be right because…'.

It is important to follow the timing of an individual child, rather than trying to explore today's question in great depth all in one conversation. In the diary I kept of my son Drew, I noted the wide range of searching questions that he asked over the year that he was four. He wanted to unravel some complex concepts, but he returned to them on several occasions within his own chosen time frame. Drew appeared to be doing a lot of thinking inside his head. On some subjects there was a gap of weeks, even a couple of months, before he asked me the next question.

I provide a personal example below, but you should hear plenty of four-year-old speculations. There are many similar examples in the practical research of Tizard and Hughes (2002) and Cousins (2003).

Expressing opinions and preferences

Generally four-year-olds like to have a one-to-one conversation or at least a discussion limited to a very small number of children with an adult. Otherwise there is too much waiting time and the conversation can take a direction that is of very limited interest to some children. Four-year-olds can manage some small group time, so long as it is sensitively led by a practitioner and this time is not the only opportunity to express their views.

Vivian Gussin Paley (2002) shared insights about the great importance of adults listening to what young children most want to discuss. Within her practice as a nursery teacher she realised that her adult plans for group discussion time were actually getting in the way. All the themes that she was trying to introduce in a structured way, arose within the children's play, especially their self-initiated pretend play. These three- and four-year-olds were not only able, but also highly

---

LOOKING CLOSELY AT FOURS

In New River Green, I was in the home corner with Clement (4 years) and Rosie (3 years). Clement moved across to a shelf on which a range of materials were easily accessible. He took a page of a magazine out of one basket. It was a complex 'maze' to join together items on a sheet featuring Rice Krispies®.

Clement wanted to explain to me in detail what was featured on the sheet. Pointing to the images of special spoons he said: "They are in the bottom of the packet. You take out the packet and they are in the bottom". He was keen for me to understand that the spoons were free gifts in packets of Rice Krispies, but were not in every packet. He explained that one day: "I brought a little Rice Krispies to nursery, but you don't get them (the spoons) in the little packets".

This example shows how children's development crosses the boundaries of areas of learning. Rosie and Clement wanted to chat, but they also showed me their confidence in using physical skills (more on page 26). I think they also showed their emotional well-being and sense of belonging in their nursery – feeling at ease to involve a visitor.

Rosie also spent time in the late morning explaining the nursery routine to me, so that I understood that lunch would soon arrive and when we could go back out into the garden.

PARTNERSHIP WITH PARENTS: VALUE CHILDREN'S QUESTIONS

Four-year-olds pose a very wide range of questions and the pattern will be an individual one. Childminders and the key person in nursery can share with families the interesting questions that a child has asked. However, it is equally important that you communicate how much you value these questions, especially the ones that make you stop and think.

Chatty and observant fours ask a lot of questions and all parents are not equally comfortable about their answers. Your approach needs to convey the message that you do not mind saying 'I don't know' or 'let's find out'. There may also be opportunities to get across that four-year-old enthusiasm sometimes outstrips social courtesies. Outspoken, top volume four-year-olds are not being deliberately rude with their public pronouncements. Sometimes they need to be guided, kindly, to saying something 'a bit personal' quietly or waiting until later.

You may also be able to share the idea of child-focused exchanges in which the adult avoids talking for ages. You answer the question relatively briefly, wait and look expectant. A four-year-old in conversation with a familiar adult will ask follow-up questions now if they want. It is not helpful if you carry on talking way beyond fours' interest in listening – especially since they started this conversation.

---

motivated, to talk about feelings, dilemmas and the enduring themes of good and bad. Much of this arose within favourite stories, some of them fairy tales, which they had chosen to rework in their play.

A small group discussion time can work, and be enjoyable, for four-year-olds so long as you tune-in to what is possible and interesting for them. Adults have to be reflective as well as realistic in what they do with the time. You also have to set an excellent example of listening and looking, as well as being the one who eases the turn taking and active respect for the views of others. Children appreciate recognition of their skills, for instance with 'Gareth, that was good waiting. I can see you were very keen to talk' or 'Katie, what a good idea, I can hear that you've been thinking hard'.

It is not realistic to expect four-year-olds to stay still for ages and their concentration, plus level of comfort, will be eased if they can sit how they like, or lay full length on the floor (sitting cross-legged for a long time on a hard floor can be uncomfortable). Emotional comfort is also important: group time should never be used to criticise children in front of their peers. Also you need to be aware that children who trust you, may talk about a very personal family issue. Show you have heard, but gently bring an end to the discussion and come back to it with this child in a confidential conversation.

For four-year-olds – perhaps for all of us – part of feeling positive about themselves is a sense of belonging and being valued. Young girls and boys need to feel cherished by their own family, but they also need to feel appreciated within their early years provision. A significant contribution is made by adults who genuinely want to hear children's opinions and preferences. It is important that experiences and routines in the provision do sometimes change as the direct result of what children have told you. Significant changes, from the perspective of four-year-olds, are not always big things from the adults' point of view. Perhaps it is a different walking route to the park or having fish pie at least twice as often.

Nurseries sometimes undertake careful consultation with young children on a specific issue, like possible changes in the outdoor area. Children can be very excited about a special project, but they gain just as much, probably more, from adults who show interest in children's views as part of ordinary daily life. As always it all depends on how the grown-ups behave.

Any invitation to children to express their opinions must involve genuine choice. Even young children soon work out that, 'they ask us but they don't listen to what we say'. They will get cross with adults who have a clear idea of what they want and are simply trying to get children to agree. You show respect to children when you are honest about decisions that have already been made by the adults, or over issues when the choices are limited in some way – maybe by time or the budget.

LOOKING CLOSELY AT FOURS

Drew initiated several conversations over the year that circled around related issues of growth for children, people's age and what was fixed and what could change over time.

Towards the beginning of that year (Drew was 4yrs, 2mths), he started with the question of: "Are my T-shirts getting small?". I had not shrunk anything recently, so I was able to say: "No" and was about to ask: "What makes you think that?" But Drew himself posed an alternative explanation: "Well am I getting bigger then? Because Tanith's got my red T-shirt now".

A world in which clothes became smaller could explain the situation. However, Drew had spotted the equally possible working theory that children got bigger. So, what had been your T-shirt, now fitted your younger and smaller sister. Over the next month or so, Drew asked questions about when you stopped growing. He was interested about whether he might end up bigger than children who were older than him. He also wanted to know if adult family members would grow any more.

Children can only generate ideas from what they know already. So it is not surprising if, given a very open brief of 'what would you like?', they tend to say they would like more, or less, of what is already familiar. They can express an opinion about new food or activities when you have organised a taster. Adult-initiated experiences can become child-initiated, once young girls and boys can base their choices on past events. When children have expressed preferences, they may sometimes question why someone else's choice was picked rather than their own. With support, and your ensuring that there is overall fairness, then young children steadily understand that this fact is part of life.

Children who feel their views are welcomed can be acute observers of daily life in a nursery or your home. Sometimes their opinions may surprise or unsettle practitioners and the comments are delivered with a four-year-old level of courtesy. Responsible adults need to reflect on what they have heard and not safeguard their level of comfort by interpreting children's honest responses as 'thoughtless' or 'rude'.

Physical development

It was a very positive change that the revised EYFS made physical development one of the three prime areas. This focus on four-year-olds' learning needs to remain very much in your mind, although at this point in early childhood you are expected to focus evenly across the seven areas. So much of children's effective learning is driven through opportunities for them to be physically active and explore within a well-resourced learning environment.

Given a choice, four-year-olds access the outdoors and many will spend most of their time in your garden or outdoor space. Best early years practice has been largely re-established with a strong focus on the value of the outdoors and easy access for children to the natural world. It is crucial that a misplaced interpretation of 'getting ready for school' (page 5) does not drag back the bizarre idea that children can only 'learn' when they are sitting quietly indoors, and that brief bursts of outdoor time are just for 'letting off steam'.

Skilled, active four-year-olds

Discussion of physical development is often sub-divided into large movements (or gross-motor development) and the fine movements, often linked with coordination between hands and eyes. Yet this distinction is not very meaningful in practice, since both broad types of movement work together.

For instance, young children need to pay close attention when they use their larger movements, and activities like climbing or bike riding need careful coordination and swift decision making. Four-year-olds can coordinate the handling, moving and lining up of equipment like ladders in a nursery or large-scale construction with blocks. They are able to work together on sustained projects such as den building with other children, and sometimes also an involved adult. On the surface, this activity may look like exclusively large physical movements. Yet the tasks actually require delicate adjustments and bodily awareness, as well as being the vehicle for a great deal of discussion.

The fine coordinations, sometimes linked with learning to write, do not operate in isolation. In fact, there are strong reasons for encouraging children in large movements that enable to become confident in balance and bodily awareness. These skills are just as important for writing dexterity – when children are intellectually able to understand what they are writing.

Four-year-olds are physically very competent, compared with their two- or three- year-old selves, but they still have much to learn and practise. They are adept at faster movements, including running. Four-year-olds usually have improved control over their movement, so that they can adjust their speed and direction most of the time. You will see the impact of earlier experience. Some children will have had plenty of opportunities for enjoyable and active play. Yet, others will have had a more sedentary earlier childhood. You will see the consequences in terms of their energy levels, as well as physical skills and confidence in movement.

Part of healthy physical development is the steady improvement in children's balance, their judgement of physical movements and their sense of bodily awareness. Four-year-olds do not need structured programmes of physical activities – unless children have a disability that necessitates specialist treatment. Ordinary active play, often outside, provides opportunities for balancing games and fours can be confident with low wall walking and clambering. The application of four-year-old balancing skills depends on what is available – equipment and activities. For instance, given the opportunity, four- and five-year-olds can learn to ice skate or ski – pastimes often associated with much older children or adults.

In order to become confident, four-year-olds need plenty of practice on what it feels like to be in balance, to begin to lose your balance and sometimes regain it after a wobble. When adults are excessively concerned about children's safety and reducing accidents to an unrealistic zero, four-year-olds may not get sufficient experience to become confident. Children use their physical skills in games, pretend play themes and for sheer enjoyment. They show greater control of skills such as jumping, with some ability to judge landing (although not always with success) and in using skills with equipment like a small size trampoline.

You will see the results of children's experience to date and also individual versions. Four-year-olds will not have perfect balance and some coordinations are still challenging for them. But you would be right to be concerned if children have persistent difficulties with physical skills that their peers approach with confidence. You may need to make sensitive adjustments for children who live with a physical or learning disability. However, the children still need to have physical enjoyment and adventures.

Children who seem highly anxious about the prospect of falling or hurting themselves may have been set on the worry path by over-protective adults. However, they may also have sensory difficulties which have not yet been diagnosed. Partial or variable problems in hearing or vision have not always been identified by four years of age. Children themselves cannot tell you there is a problem; they think a world that is fuzzy round the edges for seeing or hearing is normal.

LOOKING CLOSELY AT FOURS

In the garden of Mary Paterson Nursery School the children were able to access a range of fixed and temporary climbing structures. I watched as over one day many threes and fours clambered over a structure made up of a sloping ladder connected to a pair of horizontal planks, supported by two bases, and a slide down the other side of the plank.

This equipment was used by girls and boys alike and individual children used different strategies for going up, along and down again. Some looked more confident than others, but this variety could be observed for both boys and girls, and across the younger and eldest of the group. They all looked proud of their physical achievement and there were many calls of: "Look at me" and "I'm up".

Some girls and boys felt confident to stand upright on the planks. Some, like Jasmine (4yrs, 5mths) preferred to crawl on all fours along the plank (the two planks were put close together initially) to reach the slide. After some time, an adult moved the two top planks a bit apart. Only the most confident children continued to walk, rather than crawl, the planks with a visible gap between them. The crawlers still looked keen to try and the practitioner's action had created an appropriate challenge.

Practical use of skills

Physical skills are applied to riding three-wheeled bikes; some older fours are close to achieving the balance needed for two wheels without a stabiliser. I have seen four-year-olds who have learned the balance necessary, helped by the low slung style of two-wheeler bike, when their feet are close to the ground. Four-year-olds need to practise the sequence of skills to work the pedals in a steady forward action and also to work out how to steer round other people or obstacle courses. Bike riding requires a combination of skills that deserve respect from watching adults. Turn-taking on bikes and ensuring that keen riders do not run into other people are issues to be resolved in your outdoor area. However, I have visited many settings where such issues have been sorted with children's direct involvement.

Fours are adept at using different kinds of tools for art, craft and building. They also enjoy playing games with equipment like bats or balls. Such play combines careful looking, judgement of timing and aiming, as well as the physical actions of hitting, throwing or kicking. Learning to hit or kick a ball takes coordination and plenty of enjoyable practice. Even five- and six-year-olds are still learning some of these skills and it is especially tricky for young children to connect with a ball in mid-air.

New River Green had the practical idea of suspending tennis balls on a washing line at a suitable hitting height for children wielding a table tennis bat. They had tied a tennis ball in the foot of a series of single tights legs and tied the other end to the line. The system held the ball steady for even threes to connect with their bat. The balls returned to their hanging position, but without the disconcerting speed that comes with an elasticated line.

LOOKING CLOSELY AT FOURS

In Mary Paterson Nursery School, a group of boys worked enthusiastically with the head, for close to an hour, on the practical task of breaking up large sections of spare wood to create smaller pieces of kindling. The wood was needed to fuel the nursery fire pit ready for making and cooking pakoras in the afternoon.

The main workers on this project were Luke (4yrs, 11mths), Sam (4yrs, 9mths) and Fergus (4yrs, 7mths). They learned from the head how to prize apart a length of wood from a nailed set of planks, how to hammer down the nails safely and how to hold long planks secure whilst the work was being done. This was hard physical work and needed at least two, often three people each time, some levering and hammering and standing on the end of the plank to keep it steady. The boys worked in easy cooperation with the head and were keen to fetch tools when it became clear they needed a larger hammer.

The wood was too thick for the boys to saw through, so the head used a technique of sawing through part way and then the boys hammered to finalise the break. She showed them how to hammer close to the sawn section and held the plank secure with her Wellington-booted foot. Admiring the boys' work, she said: "You're putting a lot of weight onto that. You're making the hammer very heavy". She also introduced the idea of "we need the elephant", which was her booted foot securely down on the wood.

The boys shifted the smaller pieces of wood across to the (dormant) fire pit. They chatted as they worked, commenting and expressing satisfaction about the good job they had all completed.

WHAT ARE CHILDREN LEARNING?

There is reason to be optimistic that early years practice has largely re-established the central importance of generous time outdoors. To avoid complacency, we need to remember that tight control of outdoor time is a self-fulfilling prophecy of 'problems'.

Four-year-olds, and other age groups, are desperate to get outdoors. When their time is limited, they rush round at speed, in an attempt to pack in all their favourite activities before they are made to return inside. The intense physical activity increases the chance of crashes and battles over turn-taking. A far more relaxed timing, ideally free flow between indoors and outside, shifts the emotional environment. Children are more relaxed, they have time for sustained play or conversation and for getting a turn on a favourite item of equipment.

Outdoor play is not exclusively about physical activity, as enjoyable as that can be. There are greater opportunities in an outdoor space for being more energetic and louder, even when the garden is not substantial. Lively pretend play can expand in the outdoors. The outdoor space allows larger scale projects such as creating a den, transporting material about the garden and spreading out with a construction of milk crates and guttering.

Children, who are enthused by a shared enterprise, talk together: planning, raising ideas and problem solving. They learn, with well-judged adult support, to handle negotiation, turn-taking and delegation. In their projects they make informed judgements, decisions and learn from the consequences of their experimentation with materials.

Four-year-olds who have been given scope to practise and experiment can be skilled in the use of a wide range of tools, such as scissors, craft and proper woodwork equipment. Tool use is supported by the intellectual skills of planning and recall, as well as the communication and negotiation skills required for cooperative working with friends. Four-year-olds' improved coordination also shows in their increasing ability to share in their own care and as effective helpers in daily routines of home and nursery. Some four-year-olds will now show a definite right or left hand preference, although some will still be flexible. There is no question that adults must respect the child's preference.

Judging their own safety

With time, space and sometimes very simple equipment, children are perfectly capable of keeping themselves fit through physical activity. Their preferred playful activities are well-suited to developing their vestibular system, which is responsible in our bodies for processing our experience of gravity, position and our movement relative to what is around us.

Young children like vigorous swinging, rocking, swaying, rolling over and over and turning upside down. All these movements, which they may do with equipment or by using a playful adult as a human gym, give young bodies direct experience of balance, control and spatial awareness. These physical movements are also the ones that make some adults very edgy about safety. Of course, young children need an environment that is safe enough and adults who are serious about maintaining an environment free from avoidable dangers. However, a happy and playful childhood will not have zero accidents and over-protective practitioners or parents deny young children crucial activities for their health and future well-being.

Young children develop a sharp sense of their own bodies as the result of plenty of lively, playful activity. Their brains need to integrate the evidence of what they see, and other senses, with what it feels like to hang upside down on the climbing frame, bend double to look back through their own legs or happily have you swing them around. (You will need to watch out for the safety of your back.) If you watch fours, you should be able to see a level of confidence about their movement. With familiar activities and equipment, they have a good sense of their positioning and do not have to check visually what their limbs are doing all the time. Of course, you will see how children look and check their position when they are less sure of their next step.

Many four-year-olds are fairly accurate in their judgements of climbing and jumping. Children are less able to make safe decisions in situations where they do not understand all the factors, such as crossing the road. Temperamentally, some four-year-olds are more cautious than others, and perhaps

PARTNERSHIP WITH PARENTS: PHYSICAL SKILLS

Four-year-olds can potentially manage a range of basic physical skills. Yet individuals will apply their skills in different ways, depending on the opportunities they are offered and the choices that they make. The consideration of 'do I want to?' becomes as important as 'can I?'.

Four-year-olds are varied and some have already accepted beliefs from the adult world that affect their attitudes towards physical activity. As well as setting a good example in your own practice, it may be important to find opportunities to talk with some parents to dissuade entrenched views that some kinds of activity or games are more suited for boys than girls and vice versa.

Overly quiet children may have developed their outlook from poor practice in their previous nursery or childminder. However, what you see now may have been influenced by the atmosphere at home: that children should not engage in energetic physical activity because it is too noisy. Children, who lack this playful experience, or who have been heavily criticised, may see themselves as 'clumsy' or 'no good' at lively games.

---

always will be. Some children need to take their time, just as others benefit from your friendly 'please spot your landing place before you take off' comment. Four-year-olds are usually safe at judging what they can manage in physical skills. Problems tend to arise when they are distracted by time pressure or other children too close to them. They can also be distracted by constant cries of 'be careful, you'll fall' from adults.

Four-year-olds have considerably more awareness of their own body and ability to direct their movements in a deliberate way. Children have gained some awareness of the physical messages of their body when they make different actions. This awareness of physical feedback is called 'proprioception'. The awareness can be the source of enjoyable physical games for four-year-olds, such as deliberately spinning around to make themselves dizzy or rolling down a grassy bank. Four-year-olds make sense of some basic mathematical concepts through the direct experience of physical activity. For example, physical activity provides first-hand experiences of moving fast or slow, being close to or a long way away and the directional awareness of forwards, backwards, up and down and round and round.

Health and bodily awareness

The early learning goals for physical development in the revised EYFS talk about five-year-olds knowing the importance of physical exercise for good health. This goal is placed within the context of the strand of health and self-care, but it is still rather odd. The serious concerns about inactive and sedentary children have not arisen because young children have sat around refusing to play –but the best, most enjoyable way for them to get all the exercise they need. It has been the adults who have placed limitations on health-giving activity. Adults need to know the importance of physical exercise; children just need to be enabled to get on with it.

There has been misplaced anxiety over safety and misguided ideas about when and how young children learn. The high quality early years provision – nurseries and childminders – never stopped going outdoors and being delighted for children to enjoy active play. It is crucial now that practitioners who lost their way assign considerably more time and energy to enabling children to be active, rather than sitting around talking about healthy living in the abstract.

Much of children's understanding about bodies and bodily functions arises from conversations they want to have and questions they want to ask. Keeping clean enough and the reasons for hygiene can also develop through involvement of four-year-olds in their own daily routines, supported by simple explanations from adults. Children's interest in how bodies work shows how their desire to know supports the extension of their general knowledge. It is also a reminder that helpful

LOOKING CLOSELY AT FOURS

Some discussions about bodies arise through ordinary daily events. Getting hot or cold is of meaning to four-year-olds and they learn about ways to keep well and healthy. In New River Green, a practitioner approached one of the boys and asked: "Rory, why is your face all red? Are you hot?". The boy nodded and the practitioner suggested: "You know what might be a good idea? If you take your hat off". Rory agreed and the adult took his warm hat saying: "I'll put it on the shelf for you".

My visits to Buckingham's Nursery were spread over the summer and, it being England, some of the days were hot and some were cool and wet. I noticed many instances when practitioners reminded children, in a friendly way, about wearing their sun hat and offered help with the sun cream. On other days the adults took the time for a chat about what the weather was like and "do we need our coats today?". On one especially drenched afternoon, there was great excitement when the rain reduced to a drizzle. Children knew it was time for the Wellington boots and the umbrellas and headed outside to have fun in the puddles.

adults need to work with what has intrigued children enough today to want to ask their own questions. This approach is far more effective with under fives than pre-planned, adult-led topics about bodies.

It is undoubtedly useful to have some good quality information books that children can browse. This store will also be useful as a means to show children the answer to some of their questions. As a young four (4yrs, 1mth) my own son became interested in how bodies worked. Drew looked at the illustrations in a book about the human body and wanted to know: "How do you breathe?" and "what would happen if we didn't have bones?". He was very intrigued for some time with the picture of the human skeleton and that this structure was hidden inside all of us.

Food and social mealtimes are of great significance to threes and fours. Consultations with young children have often found that they speak up, without being asked direct questions, with opinions about the food they like and happy memories about picnics in garden. Children are far more likely to learn about food and healthy choices from genuine involvement in food preparation and meal organisation than abstract topics about 'food' or 'our bodies'.

Thoughtful early years practitioners – in nurseries as well as childminders in their family home – involve children in simple, real cooking, usually preceded by a shopping trip for ingredients. I have encountered childminders and nurseries, who have created a garden plot to grow vegetables or fruit with children. The crop has then been picked together, cleaned up and enjoyed in a meal. These experiences also support young children in learning about the natural world and a deeper understanding of the origins of food beyond the supermarket shelf.

The value of routines

Young children benefit from a pattern to their day which is predictable but not rigid. They like to know what will happen and to have some warning of a shift from one part of the day to another. Fours, and younger children too, begin to anticipate what will happen next and start to operate in an independent way appropriate to their age.

When children are sure of routines, they feel confident to organise themselves more – a skill that children will need when they enter their school years. In contrast, children are anxious when adults do not take time and trouble to manage their expectations and create predictability in the day. Children then spend precious emotional energy wondering 'is this what I'm supposed to be doing?' and 'what do the adults want this time?'. Equally, they can be unsettled by changes that happen with minimal warning.

Children need to be physically active – indeed the early years are a crucial time to lay down this particular healthy habit. Children should not be expected to sit for long stretches in their day or session. So they may well need help in the transition from active parts of the day to the few times when they do need to sit down – for meals or for a come together group time. How do you help children to cope with an inevitable transition within the day from more active times to routines in which they need to sit for a little while?

LOOKING CLOSELY AT FOURS

Windham Nursery school created a well-resourced indoor and outdoor learning environment and the children were able to move around easily. There was much careful adult planning, but it was discreet, and enabled children to enjoy free flow for most of their time. The nursery team had reflected on how best to organise their coming together time at the end of the morning and afternoon sessions.

The team had looked at the transition from freely chosen play to the one time when children were asked to sit as a whole group. I visited towards the end of the summer term, but even the older fours still needed the caring support offered by this thoughtful routine.

The shaking of a bell let children know that it was time to tidy up: a 'making things tidy' process at the end of the morning and full tidy-up at the end of the afternoon. The children were fully involved in this active work. The team had realised that many children were not then ready to move straight into sitting down inside. So they had introduced another phase: a time of physical games, such as 'Oranges and Lemons', in small groups led by adults still outdoors.

After this active period, children felt more able to go inside, enjoy a drink and some fruit. The three or four helpers of the day were the only children on the move. After this snack, children were involved in an active singing time, including using sound-makers to shake and tap in a rhythm that included a stop phase: being still as well as active.

WHAT ARE CHILDREN LEARNING?

The outing to buy ingredients for making vegetable soup was a relaxed trip and much more happened than the main plot of buying a pumpkin. In what ways do you think the following events supported different areas of the children's learning? Sachin and Beverley talked enthusiastically about their task, but also anything of interest on the way. They spotted a pile of rubbish outside a block of flats, including a big sheet of glass. They were intrigued about why the pile was there and Caroline guessed someone was having work done on their kitchen.

On the high road there was a fenced-off section with holes in the road, with two workmen standing there. The children wondered what was happening and Caroline asked the workmen. They explained that the water mains pipe was being replaced. Sachin and Beverley wanted to know about the depth of the hole and the workmen gave them an estimate.

Caroline took the opportunities for practice in how to take care crossing roads, stressing that you still had to watch out on 'quiet roads'. When we got towards the end of the outing, Beverley was able to navigate the group back to nursery.

Literacy

Older fours – and some younger fours – can be very competent and well on the road towards literacy. They can have strong foundations from the skills that will lead in time to being ready and able to learn to read and write. This section covers realistic early literacy skills to expect from four-year-olds. Unfortunately for young children, there is now an entrenched problem with developmentally unrealistic expectations with literacy ELGs in the EYFS.

The journey towards confident literacy

The demand that each five-year-old age group should be able to read and write irregular as well as common words and manage sentences was imposed on the English Foundation Stage (three to five years of age) by the national literacy strategy current at the time. Despite considerable representations from experts on early childhood and the development of literacy, these unrealistic goals continued into the EYFS and now into the revised framework, with no directly relevant modifications.

Some older fives will have made considerable progress in their reading and writing. They were ready to take this step

and experienced appropriate support, not pressure, over the earlier years of childhood. In the wide age-band of fives, some older children will reach the standards of the literacy early learning goals. However, for a range of reasons, many of their age peers – notably the summer-born children – will still be at the beginning of 'proper' reading and writing. They are not developmentally delayed and they do not have a problem, unless adults create one by branding them as failures.

English is an especially complex, non-regular language and young children need more, not less time, than their mainland European peers, to make the challenging connections between the spoken and written language. The ELGs of the revised framework are still more applicable to most six-year-olds than to most five-year-olds. Early years practitioners therefore continue to face the professional dilemma of supporting younger children with a realistic, and unharassed, learning journey towards literacy.

Fours are building up essential experience to help them understand the whole business of reading and writing. It is important to consider what four-year-olds are learning about literacy. They are developing their attitudes; this area of learning is not only about technical skills. You want children to feel and believe that reading and writing are useful skills for them and for their own future.

When there is great pressure to push young children prematurely into becoming literate, there is a serious risk that children feel they are learning to read and write solely because adults want them to achieve this skill. In a worst case scenario, children then learn to read (or write) in order to stop reading. They develop the idea that adults nag children to read, or write, and once you have done it, they will leave you alone. A different, positive set of attitudes can flourish when four-year-olds are given time to learn and to apply their skills within a practical, meaningful context. It is also crucial that they can observe familiar adults use their reading and writing skills in daily life. Then young girls and boys can be sure that literacy will open a door for them personally.

LOOKING CLOSELY AT FOURS

The head and her team at St Peter's nursery class took a thoughtful approach to written labels and other supportive materials within their learning environment. Some early literacy experiences, and the related skills of careful looking happened within the routines of the day. The backdrop of nurture was given time, because it was valued.

At mid-session drink time there were written name labels put onto mugs by one adult and today's child helper. The children identified their mug by the name. It was striking how the young threes were confident to ask the four-year-olds, if they had picked the correct mug. I observed one young child approach another girl who was busy at the writing table. The three-year-old held up her mug with the label and asked: "Is this my name?". The four-year-old girl stopped her writing, looked happy to check and said warmly to the younger girl: "Yes. Well done!".

In St Peter's (like other settings I visited) the children are active in the tidying up routine, often taking on different jobs each day. The large foam wedges needed to be stacked in one corner on shelving. Practitioners, with the children, had created a set of photos that showed several ways in which it was possible to stack the blocks. The boys who were busy in this corner were keen to show me the illustrations. They explained that the photos were needed because the blocks were a tight fit. There was a moment when everything looked chaotic. Then the head commented quietly about how was the job going and the boys checked their chosen photo and got back on track.

Oral communication and literacy

The revised EYFS has split the area of **literacy** from **Communication** and **language**. However, oral communication remains a crucial underpinning for four-year-old's journey towards literacy. Fours should have an impressive vocabulary by now and continue to learn new words through spontaneous conversation with familiar adults, and children. It is essential that young boys and girls have confident oral communication. Without this firm foundation, they will end up sounding out words, as they try to read a book, yet not recognise the word from their spoken language, when they have decoded it. Children need to know the meaning of words that they sound out from letters on the page.

Talking and thinking are crucial underpinning skills for literacy. Children who have plenty to talk about, who weigh up and plan and explore in words will have more material to write about. They still have to learn the technical skills for handwriting – and the maze which is spelling in English. However, writing needs content; it is not simply a collection of letters, however well-formed they may be. Penny Tassoni makes clear in her presentations that children could be adept copiers of a page of writing. Yet perfect handwriting skills are not the beginning and end of being a writer; content matters. Literacy is supported when four-year-olds are encouraged to talk and plan what needs to be written down. At this age children will be dictating to adult scribes.

LOOKING CLOSELY AT FOURS

The road towards literacy is supported by many aspects of children's chosen play. In New River Green, I was sitting in the home corner when Clement (4 years) was keen that Rosie (3 years) and I should work with him on a complex maze to join together items.

Rosie suggested I use my pen to complete the maze while they watched. I preferred to have an option that directly involved the children. So, I suggested that we should trace the wiggly lines with our fingers. Clement and Rosie were both confident to use their fingers to trace with care, and they looked closely to be sure of their accuracy. Between them, they explored most of the visual connections between items at different ends of the maze.

We did not use pens or pencils this time, but both children were keen to practise the sharp looking and fine physical coordination that would stand them in good stead for later handwriting.

LOOKING CLOSELY AT FOURS

Best early years practice has always used a meaningful context for young children to apply their emerging literacy skills – for reasons that make sense to the children themselves.

Louise Davies of Town and Country Kiddies described to me the normal routine in her nurseries. Each day a child used the internal phone to call the nursery cook and find out the details of the menu for the day. Children themselves then drew and 'wrote' the menu on their board.

Discussion then followed between the children about what they would be eating later and their views about the upcoming meal. Children were at ease with expressing opinions and making decisions. Another part of the usual routine was that the children made final decisions on each day about what would be laid out in some of the spaces of their nursery.

Talking and listening, within personal interactions, supports fours to build a secure understanding of the sounds and sound patterns within the one or more languages which are part of daily life to them. Four-year-olds often enjoy larking about with sounds and they pursue this by making up words of their own, or deliberately changing words and phrases for fun in their chosen play with peers. You may not be involved in this play, instead listening with a smile from the sidelines. However, your direct input will be in sharing songs, rhymes and nursery chants with young children.

Babies and toddlers love music and familiar adults singing to them. With this background of experience, fours can know a considerable number of nursery rhymes and songs. The great advantage of singing is that the words are paced in a more deliberate way than ordinary conversation; children can more easily hear the sound patterns. Many songs that you sing with children also have repeated refrains and changes in tone or emphasis which are part of the story that many songs recount. This experience sharpens children's awareness of the beginnings and ends of words, including what sounds similar, what rhymes and what does not. This development is a happy side effect of singing with children. You sing with children because they enjoy it and not to push along their literacy skills.

If you listen you will hear fours who have detailed recall of familiar songs and rhymes. Their singing or chanting shows a sharp awareness of sounds and sound making. Fours sometimes create their own version of a familiar song and play around with the sound patterns, showing a grasp of rhythm and how to rhyme words. Some young boys and

girls will only show you what they can do in small groups or one-to-one. Fours do not necessarily like large group singing times and some definitely do not want to perform in front of a group.

Love of books and stories

The ability to communicate with confidence is part of four-year-olds' enthusiasm for books, stories, storytelling and storymaking. When they have enjoyed plenty of experiences with books, fours have a thorough understanding of how books work. If you watch fours, you will see how they have grasped the basics of how to use a book from the beginning to the end. They understand the difference between illustrations and written text. Depending on their experience, some have learned conventions such as the words in a speech bubble are what someone is saying.

Over the year that they are four, many children will have grasped that English is written, and therefore read, from left to right in a side to side motion, not from right and left and not from top to bottom in columns. Children whose home language is written in a different script or direction from English may well understand the details of the difference. Monolingual English-speaking children may also understand basic differences, because they live in a community where they see different kinds of writing.

Fours know that you can enjoy books that tell a story but also that some books give you information in pictures and words. A good store of non-fiction books can have children – boys just as much as girls – choosing to pore over a book, sometimes with a friend. They use books sometimes for ideas and, with resources like an illustrated recipe book, to guide themselves in a chosen activity. I have observed fours, in provision where they have plenty of outdoors time in the garden and in trips to local parks or the beach, who confidently work with an adult to identify in a book the bird or flower that they have seen.

Fours who have enjoyed a book-rich environment have a detailed recall of familiar tales and many will tell the story from a familiar book to themselves or to a younger child. Fours are sometimes word perfect, even turning the page at the correct point. It is a positive development when children learn stories by heart, and shared storytelling is an enjoyable activity. But children need to grasp that memorising a story is not the same as reading. Practitioners need to alert parents, if they believe that a young son or daughter is an early reader, for this reason. However, it is equally important for the key person to share that this stage is to be valued as an important understanding for fours to have grasped.

Penny Munn (1997) put a spotlight on children's beliefs about reading, by asking four-year-olds basic questions about whether they could read and what they would have to do to be able to read. She asked the same children the same four questions a year later. Most of the children started the year already familiar with storybooks. But young fours believed that reading was about turning the pages and telling a story.

LOOKING CLOSELY AT FOURS

In New River Green, Clement (4 years) was busy with play dough on a table with a small group. At one point he had worked his dough into balls of different sizes. He lined them up and explained: "This is the big one and this is the medium, this is the middle size one and this is the baby one".

He placed the balls in descending order of size and then said to me that "it looks like thinking out of your head" and added "in the pictures". He indicated with his hand the "thinks bubbles" that are shown coming from people's heads. The dough looked just like that. I agreed and said: "Like the bubbles with what people say or think in pictures".

LOOKING CLOSELY AT FOURS

Fours, and many older threes, can be adept at storymaking and telling, especially with the thoughtful contribution of an adult, who follows the children's lead (Stevens, 2012).

In Start Point Sholing, I listened as a small group of three- and four-year-olds created a narrative with their key person, Beverley. She acted as a guide and a scribe. At every point, the children determined the details: the title of the story, the key characters, how the story would start, progress and how it would come to a conclusion.

Beverley encouraged with "what's going to happen next?" and wrote each stage on her clipboard. After about 10 minutes, the first story was complete to the children's satisfaction, including the arrival of fairies who saved the day. Beverley then read it back to them and the children then acted out the narrative scene by scene. Some children wanted to continue with a second story and this narrative had twists and turns. Beverley asked open-ended questions to ensure that she understood, especially over a complex scene involving ghosts, hair washing and bread, which seemed to come alive.

All the stories that children create like this one were typed up by the adults. So the children had easy access to what they have created.

By the end of the year many more children, but not all, showed an understanding that reading actually meant decoding print: that the written text was the explicit source of the story. The children's feelings about the prospect of proper reading varied. Four-year-olds who were familiar with books from their family home and nursery, appeared less daunted by realising that actually they could not yet read. Children with a family background low in literacy appeared less confident and more likely to find ways to avoid the risk of 'failure'.

From mark making to emergent writing

Young children enjoy painting and drawing and by four-years of age they can have experienced a wide range of tools and resources for making what they want to create. Their fine manipulation of different mark-making tools will mean they are closer to being able to wield a pencil effectively for writing. They may show you that they have a clear right or left hand preference. Over this year, fours with plenty of experience of mark making will start to distinguish what they tell you are their drawings and what they inform you 'says something'. This is an exciting development and shows that their meaningful mark making is developing towards emergent writing.

Fours – also some older threes – start to produce writing-type patterns because they have plenty of experience of

---

PARTNERSHIP WITH PARENTS: VALUE EMERGENT WRITING

Fours will still enjoy deliberate mark making within their more swirly creations. However, their meaningful mark making that conveys a message will steadily look more like the written form of their spoken language. Some, not all, parents may feel that this 'scribble' is not yet writing and therefore not to be valued.

In friendly conversation with parents, the key person needs to explain how the 'proper' writing will develop because children are encouraged with the letter type shapes and their earliest attempts. It is the written version of admiring and responding to a toddler's stream of expressive sound that as yet includes only a few recognisable words. You could use the term 'emergent writing' with parents or maybe call it 'scribble writing'.

You can share your knowledge with parents and other family carers with visual examples of what this individual child can do, and why it is important for literacy. Nurseries, and childminders, help this process with examples – on a board or in accessible folders – of the move from deliberately drawn patterns across a page, through mark making that looks like writing to versions that include recognisable letters from the alphabet.

LOOKING CLOSELY AT FOURS

The head and team of Mary Paterson Nursery School are committed to walking small groups of children out on a regular basis into the local neighbourhood. Apart from the particular focus for any trip, the children are always aware of information in the area communicated by words, visuals and logos. I joined a trip to walk along the towpath of the nearby canal. The children were keen to look at an information board with images of birds and other creatures that live on the canal.

They were also interested in the safety signs, such as 'Watch Out': a simple message about taking care on the towpath. We shared the towpath with cyclists and the children were especially keen to understand what the signs said about cyclists. A conversation followed, with close looking at signs and marking on the ground. The children were intrigued over how you could distinguish between signs that told you something was alright, like a designated cycle lane, and what was telling you not to do something.

LOOKING CLOSELY AT FOURS

You want young children to believe that their emergent writing is a skill that is valuable for them and one that they can apply wherever they want. You certainly do not want them to think writing is only done in a dedicated area or when adults ask children to 'do your work'.

The Grove Nursery School, like other settings that I have visited, had thought carefully about making materials portable for children. The head and her team had discussed ways to enable easy movement of materials by children from one area to another. One focus was that writing materials should not have to stay in the areas resourced especially for mark making. They wanted children to experience their emergent writing skills as something to apply with enthusiasm across the nursery.

The team had developed a range of small carrying containers, which helped children to take materials, not just for mark making, to where they needed them, indoors or outside. The containers also supported children to see materials as something to take good care of, and to return, at some point, to their main storage area.

Practitioners had personal notepads for catching informal observations within the day. These items caught children's attention and several wanted notepads of their own, which practitioners helped them to organise.

meaningful writing in their indoor and outdoor environment: notices, reminder notes that they see adults make and labels as well as the writing in books. Children also learn a great deal from going out and about in their local neighbourhood with familiar adults.

By four years of age it is very likely that children will be alert to meaningful writing on shop signs, including logos, road signs and transport directions, and the wide range of written material encountered on a shopping or other local trip. Cathy Nutbrown (Nutbrown et al. 2005) has called this important source of information 'environmental print': meaningful writing in the local neighbourhood.

Fours, especially the older fours, are likely to have a growing knowledge of the separate letters of the alphabet. However, they make sense of the world of writing from seeing examples in a meaningful context and not from exposure to single letters, without any context. Their recognition of, and attempts to reproduce, letters is usually led from experience of familiar words, such as their own name or from labels or notices that have caught their attention. Fours, and then fives, do not make one big leap into recognisable writing; they go through

several stages, which are important for practitioners to observe, and share with parents.

Fours, and some older threes, have realised that grown-ups write and they may also have watched older siblings. With easy access to pencils or crayons and time to experiment, children start to make unbroken wavy patterns which travel across the page in the direction of writing that they have seen. At this point, fours may tell you this is 'my writing'. However, they will almost certainly make this announcement at the next stage when they deliberately break up the flow of what Anne Hughes and Sue Ellis (1998) call the 'scribble stream' and form 'scribble script'. Children lift their pencil or crayon off the page and leave gaps. The pattern of marking itself may be deliberately varied.

Children are showing you through their actions that they understand writing is made up of individual symbols. Letters and letter-like shapes start to appear in children's deliberate mark making, as it becomes emergent writing. The letters start to be grouped together in word-type clusters and soon, or at the same time, fours express the wish to write a familiar word, very often their own name. Some older threes will have reached this stage. The exciting aspect of this development is that children are showing you that they have grasped that letters in a particular sequence represent a particular word. They have progressed beyond believing that a random collection of letters is the sum total of writing.

It is important to recall also that children have to grasp, at some point, that there are two broad systems of symbols: numbers as well as letters. The two different types of representation are not immediately obvious to young children. They find out through first-hand experiences with numbers in a meaningful context, often within trips out into the local neighbourhood. You also offer practical help by sorting plastic letters and numbers back into separate containers at tidying up time with the children. So, fours can have worked out that numbers are different from letters; they tell you something else and are not words.

Soon children will want to apply their knowledge of letters to write messages, notices and reminder notes such as shopping lists. Younger children may have produced meaningful marks, perhaps in pretend play and said the piece of paper was a letter from the postman. Now, however, older fours or the fives have a growing understanding of letters from the alphabet they need to make the word they want to write. As with reading, children need structured teaching to progress their specific linking of sounds to letters and letter combinations. They will take a lot of time to crack the written code of English, because for most, possibly all, spelling rules in this language there is an exception.

Young children have to tackle two related skills for writing: knowing which letters to write for each word and managing the physical forming of the letters. Handwriting requires a combination of looking carefully, holding and controlling a pencil. Four-year-olds are likely to be experimenting with different grips on a pencil or crayon and with a comfortable writing position. They need and benefit from relaxed practice with plenty of different kinds of mark making and do not benefit from being pushed into premature writing practice. When children are ready, they will reap the benefit of all their physically active play – with large, whole body movements as well as fine coordinations.

The related skill is to be able to organise in your mind what you want to write: the composition of even a short piece of writing or a notice. At this point in development you will notice the positive consequence for those children who have had plenty of experiences of creating stories with adults. When children begin to learn to write, they are often enthusiastic to write down their own stories. They are also often keen on practical applications of writing like messages, notices and shopping or similar list making. Again, you will notice those fours whose past experience has been full of joint enterprises with familiar adults, when writing (done at that point by the adult) has been applied for practical purposes which made sense to the younger child. Children draw on their past involvement now that they want to do the actual writing.

Adult literacy skills

The current anxiety about literacy has arisen because too many young people have left their school with fragile literacy skills. Some of those adults now work with young children. Fours will now be aware of writing all around them and what they see must be correct. They should never hear a familiar adult say that spelling does not matter, nor talk as if it is all too difficult to tackle. Be honest with yourself, and if those skills need some attention, then address the gap as part of your continued professional development.

It is essential that any written material visible to children, or their parents, is clearly written, or typed, and spelled correctly. Basic, correct punctuation also matters. A spell-checker on the computer will not solve the problem if it offers a correctly spelled word, which is the wrong one. It is a valuable experience for children to observe you looking closely, checking what you have written and using a dictionary from time to time. When they ask "what are you doing?", you can also explain that this handy book also explains to you what a word means.

You may judge that your own reading and writing skills are very secure. However, this issue may concern you because you support colleagues whose handwriting is illegible and spelling is shaky. You may also offer sensitive support to parents, who are motivated to address their limited literacy skills in order to read books to their young children, or be ready to help them when they start primary school.

Mathematics

Four-year-olds' grasp of early mathematical ideas is best grounded in practical problem solving, often within their play. Young children need to be allowed to make steady progress, much like their development within literacy. Familiar adults need to show appreciation of all the steps along the way and resist any temptation to push children along too fast. Overall, in the recent history of early years frameworks and official guidance in England, there has been considerably less harassment about early numeracy than over early literacy.

Amount and counting

Very young children, even the older babies, show that they have a basic understanding of amount. They show surprise, or enhanced interest, when there are more or less items in a collection that was hidden for a short while or, in daily interaction, when the toddler's attention was momentarily elsewhere. Of course, these younger children do not understand written numbers, but continued experiences have led fours to understand much more about the world of numbers and counting.

Four-year-olds can have a secure knowledge of number words, how to count and the order of numbers in the sequence up to 10, and sometimes up to 20 or more. Fours can often read and write some numbers. At a basic level, they know about number operations such as adding, subtracting and sharing out a set amount. But, the key point is that four-year-olds have come to understand these abstract ideas within a meaningful and practical context. Sometimes this context will be simple board games using dice and the need to move on your piece by the correct number. An equally important context for mathematical understanding is provided by welcoming children as active working members of your provision and letting them help in domestic routines.

Best early years practice is to establish a timing to the day that values meal or snack times and tidying up at the end of the day or session. There should be no sense of rush and then it is easy to observe how much young children learn through their competent involvement in the routine. A very great deal of practical maths happens around laying the table with the right amount of plates, beakers and cutlery. Equally, children learn a great deal from the sorting, classifying and accurate fitting that happens as they get play resources back where they belong in your accessible storage system.

So long as they have enjoyed a wide range of practical, hands-on experiences to date, four-year-olds use words for counting items one by one. Sometimes, with relatively small amounts, they may be able to say 'how many' items they have, just by looking. Four-year-olds can be relatively confident in counting 'how many?'. They need plenty of practice in number order and some four-year-olds have grasped that you count up, and down, in the same pattern each time. So six follows five each time when you are counting higher numbers.

Four-year-olds have to work out what is important and what is not. For instance, in terms of what makes something 'five', some children believe for a while that the layout of the dots on a large dice is the crucial feature. They may then argue that it cannot be five, if the dots are in a different pattern. Children are exploring what makes 'fiveness'; that the key point is how many separate items and not the exact layout of dots, or actual items.

This potential confusion for children is a good example of the need for adults to take a mental step back from what seems obvious to them. We will not spot all of their puzzlement and children benefit from working their way through some intellectual puzzles. However, sometimes fours will welcome the help that comes with "are you thinking that…?" or "how interesting, but no, it doesn't work that way".

Many four-year-olds have understood that numbers have meaning in a one-to-one correspondence, although some are still confused. Many four-year-olds with practical experience know now that, if you want five bits of wood, you stop counting at five, rather than go on and on until you run out of the numbers you know. Children have the physical skills that help them to apply their knowledge. Counting by

finger pointing, or physically moving the bits of wood, guides children to keep track of where they are in this counting task.

Just as some fours may choose to have a good try at writing letters from the alphabet, this age group will include some

LOOKING CLOSELY AT FOURS

In Mary Paterson Nursery School, lunchtime is also a relaxed and conversational time of the day. On one table it was time for second helpings and Caroline checked who wanted another sausage. She explained: "I need to know if I have to cut them. I've got 5 children who might want a sausage and only 2 sausages".

This conversation, like the similar exchange in New River Green, was calm and there was no sense of complaint from children. The exchanges are a timely reminder that fair shares and who gets seconds are very important issues when you are four years old and enthusiastic about your food.

This same table of children was also talking about numbers for very practical reasons. The conversation started because one boy had counted up the people at the table in order to know how many spoons he needed to fetch for their pudding. Other children joined in the conversation out of choice, chatting about "how many?", holding up fingers and counting.

LOOKING CLOSELY AT FOURS

In New River Green there were many times during the meal when practical numeracy mattered. For instance, dessert was tinned peach slices and some fresh fruit. Teresa was careful about sharing out the slices and the children watched closely. A friendly discussion ensued about how many slices were possible. One child said: "I want three", and Teresa explained: "We'll have to see how many there are. I'm sharing them out". Once she had gone round all the children who wanted peaches, Teresa commented: "Now I'll have some peaches. You've all got three. So there's some left for me".

A bit later one child perked up with "we haven't had seconds". Teresa explained patiently that "there wasn't enough for seconds. They've all gone. Nobody's had seconds. It's not just you". The child followed up with "why?" and the explanation was given: "Because there was not a lot of peaches today". The child repeated back "'cos there was not a lot of peaches today".

LOOKING CLOSELY AT FOURS

In New River Green I watched and listened as some three and four-year-olds chose how to use their time when they were waiting to start their meal. They decided to count up how many children there were at their table. Teresa (the practitioner) did not make the suggestion.

Rosie (3 years) could count the group accurately by pointing as she said each number. Rosie got the total correct, except that she did not count herself: a common mistake with younger children. Chris and Harry (both 4 years) were less confident about pointing with their finger and counting each individual child. The boys knew some numbers but got a little lost in the process. They did not reach an accurate total in the end but looked enthusiastic about the trying. They might well have had another go, but lunch was then ready.

As adults we have lived with a wide range of abstract ideas for many years. Mathematical ideas of number, shape, size, weight or speed may seem 'obvious' to us. However, we spent many years learning this knowledge and we need to tune into the current thinking of a four-year-old, for whom some of these ideas are far from obvious, especially in a more abstract context.

You can share your best practice in conversations with parents focused on what their daughter or son has learned this week. Highlights from their child's day can support parents to envisage what is puzzling their child about the business of counting, for instance that you stop saying numbers when you have finger pointed to all the items.

Four-year-olds build up a considerable amount of mathematical knowledge through everyday routines and games that use numbers.

Some families will already involve their children in shopping or laying the table, and play board or simple card games with them. However, parents may underestimate the value of what they are doing – especially if they believe maths is done by 'experts' in early years provision or primary school.

LOOKING CLOSELY AT FOURS

In Buckingham's Nursery I listened to a great deal of spontaneous discussion between three children who wanted to make a pretend Halloween cake with the sand. They considered their amounts, with a lot of chat around "that's enough" or "we need some more", and deciding on the appropriate containers.

A different discussion about 'enough', 'full' and 'empty' arose from the children's enthusiasm for watering the garden. The large water butt in their garden was not an endless source of water. So the children experienced that even a container this large was to be empty eventually and stayed that way until someone refilled it from the hose.

The watering cans hung on hooks fixed to the fence and this provided a regular experience for children of one-to-one correspondence because they were encouraged to tidy cans back onto the hooks.

children who are motivated to form numbers for their own practical purposes. As with letters, it is very likely that fours will not be fully accurate and that, like their letters, they may write some numbers backwards. It is worth noting that there is still no expectation, in the early learning goals to the revised EYFS, that fives will be able to write numbers. The focus of understanding is all about recognition of written numbers in a practical context. In contrast, as discussed in the section on literacy, fives are expected as a whole age group to have a developmentally unrealistic level of skill in writing letters.

Interest in size and shape

A considerable amount of early mathematical learning happens easily through the medium of play, for instance when children are enjoying resources like sand, water, piles of leaves or earth. You will hear young girls and boys spontaneously using their language to comment on or direct the play relating to position, fit, amount and size. A generous store of containers and other equipment provides fours with direct, hands-on exploration of all the early mathematical concepts that arise from filling, emptying, building and creating shapes with sand or earth.

With plenty of time for sustained play and friendly adult input, four-year-olds develop a broad vocabulary to talk about relative size and shape that make sense within their learning

environment and applied to meaningful domestic routines. They learn to look carefully and assess similarities of amount or size. Fours then choose appropriately for their building enterprise or experiment in a deliberate way. Unless they become frustrated, fours are far less likely than, say, two-year-olds, to keep jamming something into a tight space with the working theory that it will fit eventually.

However, fours can still be confused about the different aspects to a broad concept of size: height, weight and volume. You can help by being precise about the words you use. Unless we are aware, adults often use the all-purpose word 'big' to cover these mathematical concepts. The same word is also often used to cover getting older as a child: getting 'bigger' or going to 'big school'. These are not terrible adult mistakes; it is just that children benefit when we are more precise in our use of words.

Children can have amassed a lot of play experience of comparing different shapes: what is the same, what is different and in what way. First-hand experiences enable them to give the correct name to some common shapes, like square, triangle or circle. Certainly, young children are not best helped if their main experiences of shape are restricted to two dimensions on worksheets. They need to grasp that shape is also three-dimensional and can be observed all around their familiar home and nursery environments.

Understanding of different shapes is a learning journey like any other over early childhood and there is no rush. Children learn best initially through their senses. They need to see and touch the features that define different shapes and then be able to apply the words to the right shape wherever it appears. This journey will have started with babies and toddlers, who have had playful experience of baskets with a range of open-ended, safe materials. In playful times with fours, just like younger children, early years practitioners make moment-to-moment decisions about whether to comment on the play. If you over-do comments, for example about shapes or other information about mathematical concepts, you risk irritating children who feel you are taking over their play.

What puzzles four-year-olds?

Martin Hughes (1986) explored early mathematical understanding and demonstrated the impressive thinking power of four-year-olds. I realise that this research is 'old' in terms of date, but Hughes' work is well worth revisiting. He highlighted the difficulties for children in creating a bridge between their thorough informal grasp of maths and the more formal, abstract approach in primary school.

Martin Hughes showed that young children could do maths in their head but they needed to ground that thinking in familiar experiences. For instance, one of his studies showed that

LOOKING CLOSELY AT FOURS

Outdoors in Buckingham's Nursery, four-year-old Gaby had drawn a butterfly. She invited me to draw one too, so I asked her to tell me how to do it. Previously, Gaby had been shown a useful technique for building up the shapes that made a butterfly. Now she was fully able to use her words to explain to me what I had to do and in the exact order. Gaby was also confident to correct my potential mistakes, when I used my hands to make a shape above the paper to ask if this looked right to her. She used the correct words for shapes and instructed me on how to create the butterfly from several circle shapes. With Gaby's strategy I definitely produced a better butterfly than I would have done on my own.

On another day I was sitting with a small group of four-year-olds who chose to show me a set of pictures. The point was that each picture had a deliberate mistake and this was not always obvious. These young children were interested to look closely at the pictures in the set, some more than once. The children showed sharp looking skills and were sometimes able to explain why something was so wrong. For instance, one boy was very clear about why square wheels would not work on a bicycle: they would not "go round" and so the bike could not move with these wrong wheels.

well over half of the three- and four-year-olds could manage hypothetical questions about 'how many?', so long as the imaginary situation described in words made sense to the children. So, this age group could often give the correct answer to a question like 'if there were two girls in a shop and another one went in, how many girls would be in the shop now?'.

The children, even some threes, could transform the adult's words into a familiar visual image in their imagination. They often managed the correct answer, although they had nothing in front of them to count. In contrast, even the older fours struggled with abstract questions like 'what is two and one more?', which had no context at all. The puzzle was, as one four-year-old said in obvious exasperation 'one more what?'. In the intellectual world of fours, and fives too, you do not have numbers floating around, unattached to anything at all.

Penny Munn (1997) explored four-year-olds' understanding of counting: what it was and whether they could already count. Her research into the four-year-olds' world of numeracy is a timely reminder that adults need to look through children's eyes. Young children initially confused saying and reading the numerals with actual counting. There are parallels for four-year-old beliefs about literacy: that retelling a story is the same as reading. Over the period of a year, children largely came to understand that, in order to count, the numbers needed to be linked with items. Munn observed that this understanding became established when young children applied their ideas in play led by their own purposes – not disconnected worksheets. Practical counting also made sense within shared routines where children had an active role in collaboration with their peers and with adults.

Four-year-olds need to see the practical applications of numbers and other mathematical operations. They need a sense that numbers are all around them: a mathematical version of Cathy Nutbrown's idea of environmental print (Nutbrown et al., 2005). Maths is more than numeracy and young children need steadily to build a bridge of understanding between the practical and the abstract. They are helped when adults – practitioners and parents – use mathematical talk in a natural way. Just as you comment sometimes on what you can see, you can voice your mathematical thoughts out loud. Of course you do not talk all the time, but you make comments

LOOKING CLOSELY AT FOURS

In Buckingham's Nursery I noticed many instances when an adult commented briefly and appropriately on what the children were doing. But sometimes, the adults focused on playing without making this kind of comment.

I watched an enthusiastic game when an adult and several children were stepping carefully around the outline shapes marked on the flat surface. The adult did not comment on the shape they were walking. I think she was right, because the fours, and threes, were concentrating on walking the triangle and the other shapes with precise steps.

On another afternoon, I watched another energetic game, this time where children were keen to roll hoops – not an easy task until you have practised the technique. Boys and girls were persistent, and occasionally successful, in rolling a hoop along the ground. The adult rolled four or five hoops at the same time – a striking effect – and at a 'ready steady go' from her the children ran after them.

This fun activity provided direct experience for children of the operation of a plaything that is circular. Again the practitioner focused on the enjoyment of a lively running game, and I think that was appropriate. Active children were busy with direct experience of what happens when a circular shape is rolled.

LOOKING CLOSELY AT FOURS

Fours can be enthusiastic and competent cooks, especially if they have been introduced to recipes and food preparation from a young age. Cooking is an excellent joint activity with young children – plenty of practical maths and something nice to eat at the end. In Mary Paterson Nursery School some of the cooking is done outdoors with a fire pit. I watched as two adults and several children were busy setting up ready to prepare and cook potato pakoras on the fire pit.

The food preparation was led by Shamila and five children were closely involved throughout. They had helped to organise the table, bowls and a chopping board. They were making potato pakoras. Shamila explained each stage of the recipe and ensured the children could smell the different spices. The children were keen to talk about the different ingredients. Shamila explained that the flour was chickpea flour and not ordinary wheat flour. Most of the children knew what chickpeas were. When anything was needed, individual children went off to fetch it, for instance for more vegetable oil and a bowl of water.

A lively conversation started about other cooking that they had done outdoors in the past. Three boys reminisced about when they cooked the fish on the fire. They recalled how they had cleaned it, explaining to other people that it was "a dead fish" and how an adult cut it up and they cooked and ate it.

like 'I wonder if this will fit? Could we measure it?' when you are building with children or 'I think something's missing' as you look together at the snack table and you know there are not enough cups or forks.

Money is a complex part of mathematical thinking, yet four-year-olds have some understanding, as well as confusion. Part of understanding money is about the numbers, but money value is more complex. For young children to understand money, they need to grasp the symbolic function of coins and notes. Part of their learning is dealing with the illogical fact, from children's perspective, that the largest coins are not necessarily those with the highest purchasing value. Sometimes a smaller pile of coins will buy more than a large pile.

Four-year-olds can be very competent in managing the number work involved in money, so long as have a realistic situation through which to connect what they know so far. Some of their explorations are through play and you will hear some lively exchanges in a pretend shop or post office. However, paying for pretend cakes in their café or putting the prices on a menu will not be sufficient. Young children also need first-hand experiences of paying for real items with real money, supported by a familiar adult, for instance in shopping trips. Four-year-olds learn from accompanying adults – parents as well as practitioners – on high street trips to the banks or post office. They witness the use of cash machines and take another step in trying to grasp money ideas, when cash appears in an almost magical way.

Four-year-olds can surprise adults in the extent they understand money and value, when the application is part of a practical discussion. Children can be involved some of the choices for spending money in their early years provision. Judy Miller (2003) gives the useful example of a group of two-, three- and four-year-olds, who helped to choose play resources from a catalogue for their crèche. The children were told the budget limit and they had the same number of discs as the total pounds limit. The practitioner supported the children as they offered choices and then counted out the number of discs that they would have to pay for this item. These young children could see how much 'money' would go from their budget in order to pay for particular items. They were able to discuss, and move pretend coins to and fro, until they reached an agreed shopping list. A smaller group of children made the trip into town with a practitioner and purchased the toys that had been agreed by the whole group.

Judy Miller's work provided many good examples for practitioners to adjust for their own provision. I have encountered similar examples within my training days. Early years practitioners have taken simple steps, such as using visuals, to enable under-fives to make sense of otherwise rather abstract ideas. I have been told about vegetable plots and other gardening projects, where young children were brought fully on board about how much money was available for buying seeds and plants. Fours and fives also became

skilled at working out what 'we can ask people to give us', so that the limited amount of money was spent wisely.

Apart from the valuable practical maths, these joint projects with children gave the valuable lesson that adults do not have endless supplies of money. Choices need to made: between one big plant or item of equipment and several smaller ones.

Four-year-olds rarely understand clock time and it is not unusual that six or seven year olds are still confused with telling the time. But an understanding of time is much more than clock time and adults can support young children as they understand this concept. Four-year-olds learn about the concept of time through familiarity with routines. Pleasantly predictable routines enable them to understand the sequence of events within a day or session and the meaningful passing of time. Four-year-olds understand time related to what can be fitted into a time slot, like one more circuit of the garden on the bike, before five minutes makes much sense. They also understand the use and value of simple time measuring devices such as large sand timers or setting an old style egg timer that will 'ping'.

Four-year-olds' language also begins to reflect the vocabulary of time with words and phrases for parts of the day like morning and afternoon and time indicators such as 'soon', 'later on', 'when can I..?' and 'how long will you be?'. You help by avoiding over-use of "Just a minute", if only because enterprising fours will set the timer on you.

Understanding the world

Two significant strands of rethinking of best early years practice have benefited young children in recent years. One strand has been the serious professional reflection about flexible planning. Forward plans that genuinely work for young children rest upon practitioners' knowledge of individual children: their current interests, what they are motivated to explore this week and what is likely to intrigue them. There has been a significant move away from adult-led, pre-organised topic work, in which most, if not all, of the details have been planned well in advance.

The other very positive change has been the rediscovery of the value of the outdoors and plenty of time for children outside. Some nurseries and childminders never lost this vital focus. An over-organised day and a narrow view of learning that sidelines the outdoors will disrupt positive experiences for children in all the areas of learning. The imposition of pre-packaged knowledge seriously undermined some young children's enthusiasm for learning about their world.

What do fours want to know?

Young children, even babies, show you what interests, or puzzles, them by their behaviour: what they do, the choices they make and all their non-verbal communication. The exciting development with fours, and many older threes, is that they are able now to use their spoken language to ask questions and make questioning type comments. This information is vital for guiding adult behaviour; the focus needs to be on what questions do the children ask today and not on what questions the adults think are important.

Barbara Tizard and Martin Hughes (2002) and Jacqui Cousins (2003) offered many examples of the searching questions that fours ask, when they are in a relaxed environment with adults they trust to be interested and helpful. I was further provoked to think about adult behaviour with young children when I visited Saplings Nursery in

South London. Their development team had a useful set of questions about questions, which I paraphrase below.

Do you consider sometimes: 'Is this a genuine question that I am asking?'. A good way to check is to ask yourself:

● Do I really want to know the answer from the child(ren)?

● Do I already know the answer?

● Does the child have the answer and I do not?

It is well worth considering: 'Do I ask a lot of questions?'. Equally you need to reflect on: 'Do I ask a lot of testing questions?'– questions to which you already know the answer, but you want to see if the children can give the correct reply. Testing questions are a very narrow form of communication with children. The more adult questions they hear, the less young boys and girls are likely to volunteer their own – more important – questions. Additionally, testing questions may bear little relationship to individual children's knowledge and interests. Some fours may want to co-operate, but they are confused about what you are asking. You need to take notice of their puzzled expressions and when they give you 'odd' replies. The overall message is that you are talking non-sense, in terms of this child's current knowledge.

Exploring the local community

Fours are curious about their world and some young boys and girls will show you that they already have an impressive

LOOKING CLOSELY AT FOURS

During the shopping trip from Mary Paterson Nursery School (see page 23), there was time for Sachin (3yrs, 9mths) and Beverley (4yrs, 3yrs) to look at other aisles and they homed in on the meat counter. They were intrigued to know what was in the different packets. Beverley thought the packaged chickens were 'piggys' but Sachin was sure they were chickens. But their conversation also explored that the chicken looked bare, not like a normal chicken and "why is there blood?". Caroline explained that the meat had been live animals originally.

They looked at chicken legs on the way and a bright red chilli plant – they agreed with Caroline that the chillies were hot – too hot for children. They were also interested in the packaged fish and what were they? Caroline told them the names by reading out the labelling of any package. They looked at a packet of swordfish and Sachin said: "It looks like a shark". Caroline agreed: "It does looks a bit like a shark".

PARTNERSHIP WITH PARENTS: WHOSE QUESTIONS?

You may be able to share the practical ideas with parents about asking genuine questions. Parents too can sometimes find themselves asking testing questions of their children – with good intentions that this pattern will support young learning.

You can also, in partnership, show your respect for the questions that four-year-olds want to ask. The example in this section gives only a few of the issues that intrigued my son over the year that he was four. Perhaps, with parents, you track the children in your setting, noting their questions and queries. You will find similar examples of the lively thinking and curiosity of four-year-olds about the world around them.

LOOKING CLOSELY AT FOURS

My son, Drew, asked a considerable number of questions as a four-year-old. Within this year, Drew started to watch the children's programme 'Newsround'. He was concerned about the famine at that time and asked "why are the people hungry in Ethiopia?". The explanation that they had no food led to a logical second "why?". Drew realised that some of what he could see on television was actually happening and some was just a story. He wanted to work out what was real and what was not and he created his own question, to ask whether an event or a person was 'in this world'.

Drew was interested in the natural world. He had been keen to look up at the 'moon and stars' since he was a very young two and our winter afternoon walk back from his childminder was in the dark. As a four-year-old, he wanted to find out about stars, planets and how come astronomers could study the sky. His interest was supported by reference books that he was given for his own shelf or that he chose to get out of our local library. Drew was also interested in the weather and how it came about. I did not have easy answers to many of his questions, such as "why do you get a double rainbow?" after we had seen this amazing sight one afternoon.

Over this year, Drew asked many questions about babies, birth, how people got ill and who could die. I learned to answer briefly and avoid talking beyond the point where my answer was enough for what he wanted today. Like many young children, Drew sometimes left days, even weeks, between his questions on the same broad topic.

knowledge base. They learn through direct, first-hand experiences – going out and about with familiar adults in their local neighbourhood. Their knowledge has to start with their immediate world and stretch outwards from the familiar to the less familiar. Books and other information resources can be very useful, including careful use of the Internet, but they have to link with children's current interests and knowledge base.

Developmentally appropriate practice is that early years practitioners extend young children's knowledge of the world from their personal life and immediate local community. Under-fives struggle to make connections of meaning to people, places or events that are utterly unfamiliar to them, regardless of whether these are normal life for families who live in other parts of the UK. There will always be some kind of diversity in the local early years provision, but it will not always be that of visible ethnic differences. In what ways could you draw on aspects of your local neighbourhood? In what ways does your local population vary?

LOOKING CLOSELY AT FOURS

Many families whose children attend Mary Paterson Nursery School are originally from Morocco and Bangladesh. One long-term project with the children was to convert the small room within their indoor environment into 'Morocco'.

The room was changed with appropriate resources. Children helped in the transformation, going out with practitioners to buy fabrics. Everyone had to show a passport to go into the room over this period. Children had made the passports as part of an ongoing interest in different kinds of documents. This internal facility was supported by outings to shops in the immediate neighbourhood which sold Moroccan produce.
The outings were then extended to shops run by Bangladeshi families. The children then had a trip on public transport across London to Brick Lane, in the east end, where they went to a restaurant and enjoyed a Bangladeshi meal. The nursery takes groups of children to a local café or restaurant for occasional outings.

This long-term project of exploration rested on the direct experience of some children, in terms of their family background. However, it also made sense to those children whose background was neither Moroccan nor Bangladeshi, since what happened in their Morocco room was connected with local sights and experiences. It was possible to extend the nursery children's learning with an appropriate DVD, but their understanding had been grounded in first-hand experiences in the first place.

Unnecessary restrictions on outdoor play have often arisen from adult anxiety. A more robust approach to risk assessment has been part of re-establishing the importance of the outdoors and respecting children's need for adventurous activities. The revised EYFS, and the much reduced welfare requirements, have taken further helpful steps in making it clear that early years practitioners are responsible for making considered judgements about how to keep young children safe enough, without blocking valuable activities.

Of course, early year provision will vary in what is within walking distance in the local neighbourhood, as well as the natural environment of your outdoor space. Yet, there will always be something to see, and young children are interested in the ordinary possibilities, like going to your nearest open green space or getting books out of the library. Fours are intrigued by road works and building sites, which are only dangerous places to children if they cross the outer boundary. Diggers, cranes and all the paraphernalia of a building site can be viewed from a safe distance: another enjoyable local trip I took with a group from Mary Paterson Nursery School.

Four-year-old emotional literacy (see page 7) is also about their readiness to be thrilled and enchanted, especially in contact with the outdoors. They are intrigued by natural materials of mud and water, by magical sights like a rainbow or a clear view of the stars and the endearing antics of baby

LOOKING CLOSELY AT FOURS

The nursery garden in Mary Paterson Nursery School contains a fire pit and children learn how to be safe when the fire is lit. The head and three boys had worked hard preparing wood in the morning (page 20). In the afternoon, the final preparation was to consider safety measures, ready for lighting the fire pit for cooking.

Several children went with Maria (a practitioner) to get a bucket of sand. The boys filled a bucket from the outdoor sand pit. Luke (4yrs, 11mths) took it across and placed it within the (unlit) fire pit area. Another child had gone to fetch a bucket of water. Another adult explained to watching children that they needed the sand and water to put the fire out properly when everything was finished.

Luke and Josh (3yrs, 3mths) helped Maria to break up sticks for the fire. They worked to pile up the wood inside fire pit until there was enough and Maria was ready to light it. Once the fire started to catch, the boys went off to find dry leaves, "some scrunchy ones" and Maria agreed that would be useful.

LOOKING CLOSELY AT FOURS

I joined a group of threes and fours from Mary Paterson Nursery School on a local trip to the Grand Union Canal. The children walked non-stop (happily) for over one-and-a-half hours. The adult plan was to reach the houseboats on the canal, but the practitioners' timing allowed for unplanned sights of interest. The children had the opportunity to check out the road works on the high road: deep holes in the road and working diggers. On the way out their attention was caught by a black cab limping along with a noisy flat tyre and on the route back to nursery we were lucky to spot two men cutting branches off a very tall tree.

The walk along the towpath gave relaxed opportunities for children to spot the water birds, work out the difference between ducks and swans and wonder what they ate. They looked for signs of fish and speculated whether the canal would have sharks. It was a breezy day and one practitioner pointed to the ripples on the surface of the canal. She explained that the wind was making these little waves. Children commented on the effects of the wind twice later, further along the towpath.

We watched as the first narrow boat came along the canal, waving at the people on board, and a practitioner explained that these boats were people's homes. The children were intrigued to look closely as we then passed many boats moored to the towpath. They chatted about why there was a rope tied tightly to hold each boat and pointed out the features they could see. The children were interested to hear that all these boats had a kitchen and bedroom, just like any home.

birds or animals. Four-year-olds are delighted; they are far from cynical because the world is still new to them.

Familiar adults need to respect and support children's sense of wonder and their wish to enjoy, look and listen. You will support their learning in the broadest way when you join children in what they want to show you. Best early years practice is that you are led by children's current interests and fascinations: here is the cutting edge of their learning. Four-year-olds are far more likely to listen and learn from adults who have a good track record of showing genuine interest in what has caught the child's attention and in what way.

Four-year-olds are keen to watch how worms wiggle into the crumbly earth or how the condensation forms on the window. They are poised to learn from this first-hand experience. Resist the temptation that you should provide information or explanations straightaway. Young children may love to build a worm house, but not right away. Also it is wise to hold back on asking questions that you think are important. Be guided by children and focus on those questions they want to ask. It is helpful to make comments that show you have noticed the details and are pleased the child has brought this interesting sight to your attention.

Fours, and any young children, depend on their familiar adults to provide accurate information. It is, of course, fine to admit that you do not know and follow with "but let's find out". It is also fine to let a child know that their working theory

– about bones or where slugs live – is an intriguing and good guess, but on this occasion not correct.

Sometimes children want to explore and find more information right at this moment, but often not. You will help by remembering what you shared and helping a child to make connections at a later date. You might suggest a way to explore how condensation gathers or that you could lift the log in the garden, because that is a likely home for little creatures. It is just as important that you let children know that you have not forgotten by reminiscing: "I was remembering when we…".

Technology

The wording of the revised early learning goals for the end of the EYFS has usefully strengthened the message that children's learning about technology is not all about computers. A considerable amount of four-year-old current

Children enjoy working the machines that belong to grown-ups, and they understand that in some cases this experience will be with adult supervision.

In the Grove Nursery School several children had been closely involved in a writing project linked to the hairdressers' role play area that they wished to create. Children had discussed and helped to draft a letter for parents that explained their plans and made a request for a list of items to stock the hairdressers. They then used the nursery photocopier, with adult support, sorted out the letters and stood and handed them out to each parent at pick-up time.

In Windham Nursery School the children also knew that they could ask to use the photocopier, accompanied by an adult. The well-resourced writing area – outdoors as well as inside – had a store of little whiteboards.

Whenever children wanted a copy to keep of what they had drawn or written on their board, they just asked for a trip to the photocopier.

and growing knowledge in this area is focused on everyday technology, familiar from their home, your home as a childminder, nursery and in the local neighbourhood.

Four-year-olds are interested in 'grown up' technology that they can access through their play and use within their imaginative play. They enjoy playing with mobile or landline phones (with batteries and sim card removed). However they also appreciate using a proper phone or a walkie-talkie. It is now common in early years provision for children to have access to a camera, sometimes a disposable version. In any provision that I have visited, the four-year-olds, and the threes with adult help, show care and respect for what they recognise as special equipment, not a plaything as such.

Interested fours are enthusiastic to learn practical techniques and usually accept friendly advice, so long as they are given scope for safe experimentation. Many settings, and some childminders, have invested now in a digital camera and young children are involved not taking some of the pictures. Some fours become adept at working with images on the screen and knowledgeable about what their system will do. Four-year-old girls, as well as boys, can be sharp at noticing what a new system will, or will not, do for them in comparison with the system with which they are familiar.

Even if adults are not yet at ease to hand over the digital camera, children should be fully involved in deciding what

should be done with the images: for their own portfolio, the wall of their room or a large book about their project or a shared outing. I have now also encountered nurseries (Buckingham's Nursery being one of them), which have a laptop set up in the open area to the nursery with the current set of photos running as a display for parents. Within my training days I have spoken with childminders who have set up the same facility in their home.

Four-year-olds are interested to look at technology that is common on the high street and they build their understanding through local trips. They like to operate the controls of pedestrian crossings, which also forms the vital experience that – slowly over more than early childhood – will be part of their learning about safety around roads. There can look at, and sometime watch adults use, the cash and credit card machines in banks and post offices.

As well as regular trips out and about locally, you may be able to organise in advance with the manager of a local shop or restaurant for a small group to be shown how the checkout operates or what lies behind the CCTV cameras.

Children benefit from visiting the local library on a regular basis, where they can become familiar with the screen and scanning system for taking out and returning books. There could also be opportunities for you all to use the library database to search for favourite authors.

Fours and younger children are interested in domestic appliances, like a cooker and washing machine, and how they work. In their family home or that of their childminder, young children have opportunities to understand the basics of how this technology works. Appropriately for their age, they start to be involved in pressing some buttons and dials, supported by an adult. This practical knowledge is part of children's growing understanding of the world. Also, you cannot teach children how to behave responsibly around machinery or sources of heat, such as in a kitchen, if you never let them have access.

The revised EYFS has reduced the pages of welfare requirements. One useful change is the disappearance of the previous requirement on group provision to keep children out of the utility room or kitchen under all circumstances. All practitioners are, of course, required to maintain a safe environment and act so as to keep young children safe. However, the revised statutory framework now effectively trusts all practitioners to make wise choices about when children could, with an adult, be actively involved in loading up the washing machine or cooking in the kitchen during quieter periods of the day in group provision.

Children may sometimes wish to extend their interests and self-chosen projects by using Internet resources as well as books. Familiar adults – practitioners and parents – need to be computer literate and Internet confident, because this

area of learning is not only about the technical aspect of how to get into websites. Young children need you to guide them about how they could research possible answers to their question. (Any computer available to children should have software installed that will block access to unsuitable sites.) However, as soon as adults invite children to use the Internet for any kind of research, you need to be a friendly presence to chat about how far this information answers our question, does it make sense and do we need to look for another source as a check.

There must be no sense of pressure on young children to get on the computer. They have plenty of time throughout their later childhood, and adolescence, to explore computer technology in detail, along with all the changes that continue to evolve. Responsible adults ensure that children are fully confident with using the low-tech approaches of emergent writing and using numbers, drawing by hand and not simply downloading ready-made artwork. Children need to continue to use books as well as being able to access websites and, with your help, judge the quality of information they find there.

Some child-led projects may benefit from using a word processor function or simple number layouts and charts. Children may be keen that you type up a neat version of their

LOOKING CLOSELY AT FOURS

Alongside learning about how to operate common technology, children are also fascinated by how appliances work. With care, their curiosity can be satisfied.

When I visited Grove Nursery, the permanent play provision included a technology table, resourced with old telephones, cassette players and anything mechanical or technological. The batteries had all been removed. The table was equipped with proper tools, like screwdrivers and wire cutters. The children were encouraged to take a look at what was inside some of these familiar items. I was genuinely intrigued as one four-year-old girl adeptly took apart a telephone to show me the hidden parts. I was able to say, honestly, that I had never seen the inside of a telephone before.

In Windham Nursery School, one family had donated an old video player. Over the entire summer, this equipment was left on a table with tools. The children took it apart bit by bit. When I visited towards the end of the term, the deconstruction was almost complete. Children were proud to show a visitor what they had done and discovered about the insides of a video player. They also fully understood, like the children in Grove, that you did not take a screwdriver and cutters to working machinery.

story or recipe, which they can print out and further embellish. The outdoors will give more space for using programmable toys. These can be a useful resource, but again should not take the place of low-tech constructions that the children are enthused to make from recycled materials.

Iram Siraj-Blatchford and John Siraj-Blatchford (2003) emphasise that under-fives can steadily develop what they call an 'emergent technological literacy'. Children extend their knowledge of the many different uses of information and communications technology. Appropriate activities, adult guidance and well-chosen equipment – not least the placement and seating arrangements for a computer – will support children's practical skills to access the opportunities of computers, whilst minimising the drawbacks of over-use. These two writers also advise strongly against using time on the computer as a reward, or withdrawing this opportunity as a consequence of disruptive behaviour. The computer should be treated like any other resource in nursery or a childminder's home and not as something special.

Adults – practitioners as well as parents – have to take the responsibility to ensure that children do not spend ages looking at a screen. You cannot expect children to monitor themselves. However, given a well-resourced learning environment, you will not necessarily have to prise every child off the computer. A certain amount will depend on their experience so far elsewhere, or in their family home. It is best to locate the computer within the main space and not in a separate room. You want to give the message to fours that the computer is a source of information and exploration that works alongside their other skills and knowledge.

The parallel adult responsibility is to ensure the high quality of any computer software made available in your provision. Like any resources for children, you should not simply trust the packaging or marketing. Some software could well work to complement plenty of first-hand experiences. However, I have watched young children on some allegedly educational software, which gave a considerably less challenging and rich experience than they would have gained from active play with suitable resources.

PARTNERSHIP WITH PARENTS: TECHNOLOGY IS NOT ALL COMPUTERS

Early years practitioners need to set a good example in careful use of computers or related equipment with young children. A section of the toy industry is very keen to market this kind of technology as allegedly the best way for young children to learn, even to promote computer-type technology for babies.

The key person will be able to share all the different ways that fours use technology. You will share with parents not only the current understanding of their son or daughter, but also the message that young children should be using computer and related technology for good reasons. More time looking at a screen does not necessarily equal greater learning.

Your anecdotes should easily include examples of what practitioners within the Steiner Waldorf approach to early education call 'warm technology'. This phrase refers hand-held beaters, drills and other tools not fuelled by electricity. With a bit of guidance, these tools are soon safe for independent use by fours.

Expressive arts and design

Young children have a fresh outlook on life that sets them up well for creativity. Fours are very open to possibilities and have an enthusiasm for using ideas and materials in whatever way works. Creative development can be supported by child-friendly arts and crafts, but creativity also flourishes through imaginative play and the buzz of independent thought.

An environment to encourage creativity

Fours are supported in a well-resourced learning environment that enables them to make genuine choices. Best early years practice for children is also that knowledgeable adults take a flexible approach to planning, including time and timing. Four-year-olds, and younger or slightly older children, cannot express themselves, if their explorations are firmly bounded by practitioners' decisions about length of time and location. Of course, you have to have considerate time management; there

is an end to the day or session. Yet, there is no reason why a project that enthuses children should not last days or weeks and this happens now in many settings. It is also important to consider where children will spread out with a project that needs generous space or sometimes more than one location, especially when fours are keen to use a wide range of resources.

It is important that practitioners value the process and do not get fixated on something to show at the end, whether in a display or to give to parents. However, the end product does matter, as the behaviour of young children will often show you. They can be excited and proud of what they have managed, but they can also be disappointed and frustrated. Familiar adults need to be sensitive, listening to children and looking at their personal reactions. Does this four-year-old want to have another go, and would appreciate your practical help? Does this other young child want your fellow feeling that it is so annoying when all that hard work does not pay off – but the project is over, at least for today?

A mixed group of twos, threes and fours in St Mark's Nursery School enjoyed having buckets of water and paintbrushes in the garden on a warm summer's day. The children were given a free choice about how to use the materials and had been very involved in the organisation of these resources.

The younger children were fascinated by simple brushing onto the paved surface. They were interested in how the water disappeared in the heat of the day. The slightly older children experimented with the chalks that were also available. Some of them chose to chalk around the water, and then watched as the wet area retreated and shrunk. Their chalked outline was a clear indication of how far the wet area had dried out.

Children returned to these resources over the afternoon. As well as relishing their outdoor artwork, these young children had extended their understanding of a familiar world through a practical exploration.

Children are undoubtedly very pleased to see their painting or a photo of their outdoor twig sculpture in pride of place. But they need to be able to make their own decisions about what they make and when they have finished. It can help if adults reflect on their own attitudes to the wall space. When I visited Windham Nursery School, the team had significantly reduced the number of display boards in their setting. On reflection they decided that large areas of wall space put the pressure on adults to children to make paintings, collage and other project work that would cover the walls.

Of course, display does not have to mean flat wall space; some models or works in progress need shelf space. The team at Windham, and other nurseries I visited, have thought in a very creative way about how to display what young boys and girls have done, in active cooperation with the children themselves. It is not always necessary to tidy up a project at the end of the day. I have visited nurseries that use 'work in progress' notices, so that a large construction can be left over several days.

This option is not available to the packaway settings, who share their space with other service users. Taking photos is a practical answer and, in any provision, some large projects can be 'kept' in the end by enabling children take photographs. However, there is no need to feel pressure to document everything; sometimes there is simple pleasure for everyone in relishing the flow of the play.

In a friendly atmosphere many four-year-olds will be happy to speak up in small group times and to contribute a song or rhyme. But there is nothing to gain and much to lose by putting any pressure on children. It is guesswork to explain a child's refusal in terms of 'shyness'. Some children simply do not want to 'perform' in a large group – although some are delighted. The allegedly 'shy' children are often perfectly comfortable and communicative in one-to-one or very small groups. Fours often enjoy dancing and do not necessarily need an involved adult – just some space and suitable music. In a happy atmosphere, fours will now also use their singing and musical skills in spontaneous events of their own choosing.

Tools, techniques and safety

It is also worth reflecting on different kinds of end product. Something important for children and the involved adults may emerge, but it will not always be tangible. The significant outcome for children may be a warm memory that they return to many times later in conversation. An important outcome for them can also be 'getting much better' at a skill. Four-year-olds develop in technical skills, but also in the personal satisfaction that develops from being able to make choices of technique, materials and style.

The crucial role for adults is to provide plenty of resources and be a helpful presence, ready to guide when appropriate. It supports four-year-olds to understand that everyone gets better with practice. Adults were not born knowing how to sew, wield a hammer or make towers that do not collapse. Older children, who appear 'so good' at drawing their spaceships have spend a lot of time honing their technique on their chosen images.

Sometimes the most important priority is that the adults address, and put to one side, their sense of pressure that children must produce something on a regular basis. The pressure particularly undermines creativity if there is a sense that all children must produce something similar. Under these circumstances, the adults all too often do much of the work – beforehand or afterwards. Any artwork or other creations have to be children's work, otherwise there is no point. The problem with very structured activities, in which children are directed to make a card or a model 'like this', is that

LOOKING CLOSELY AT FOURS

Ben and Clement (both 4 years) were at the dough table in New River Green. These boys and two other children (both 3 years) were absorbed with the play dough for a long period. They talked about what they were doing, looked at what their companions were making and sometimes chose to imitate. What else is going on in this example as well as a creative endeavour?

Clement showed me how he had cut out a star shape. He lifted out the star shaped dough, but was equally interested to show me the clear empty shape that was left. He explained: "Because if you have a star shape you have one left". He wanted to count the arms of the empty star but had difficulty counting round each arm and arrived at three each time he tried.

Then, Clement had rolled his dough but it had stayed tight wound around his roller. He found this amusing and I said: "That's what sometimes happens to my pastry when I cook at home". The other children imitated Clement and worked hard at getting their dough to wrap around the roller and stay firm.

Three out of the four children were now rolling their balls into different sizes. Ben explained his set: "This is the Daddy one, this is the Mummy one, this is the sister one and this is the tiny one". Clement now described his as: "A Daddy one, a Mummy one, a brother one and a sister one".

Clement then rolled up his dough (not around the roller this time) and explained: "This is going to be a carpet rolling up and you roll it back out again". The other children now tried their own 'carpets' with the dough.

LOOKING CLOSELY AT FOURS

At New River Green it was tidying-up time before lunch. The children gathered in one part of the nursery space and the tidying tasks were shared out. Children went off to different corners of the room and set about their tasks. I stayed with the three children who were tidying up in the home corner.

They were busy chatting as they tidied up and were capable of talking and tidying efficiently at the same time. Clement (4 years) said with excitement: "We're going to have some lunch today!". A second child repeated the phrase and spontaneously they made it into a song, like a refrain. The three children sang: "I need some lunch, we're having some lunch, we always have some lunch" and they repeated the 'verses' several times very tunefully, as they continued with their tidying task.

This example shows children's ability to concentrate and do more than one thing at the same time, especially when they have a clear practical task in a familiar context and they are motivated to complete it. Yet, I think the sequence also shows how young children, who feel happy, will break into spontaneous song. In this way, singing can well be viewed as an indicator of emotional well-being.

LOOKING CLOSELY AT FOURS

Sometimes children are fascinated by an art form that they are unlikely to manage themselves. In New River Green a mixed group of three and four-year-olds were well able to watch and wait in a friendly atmosphere with interest and the chance to chat. They were waiting their turn on a hand-painting activity offered on the outdoor veranda.

One practitioner and an older child, present for the summer holidays, were doing designs on the back of children's hands if they wished. The children were able to choose from several possible designs and then select the colours they want.

The two children being painted at any one time were able to stay very still while the design was painted. Yet the surrounding small group of three and four-year-olds was also able to be patient. They watched intently as the designs were painted, talked about what design they might want when it was their turn and pointed to the colours in the unusual little pots. They were also interested to quiz the older child to whom the materials belonged. One child wanted to know "is that your own brush from home?".

PARTNERSHIP WITH PARENTS: ADVENTUROUS AND SAFE ENOUGH

Grandpont Nursery School had found that if parents were going to be uneasy about any nursery activity, it was most likely to be about the prospect of the woodwork table. When parents and their children came for the first visits, practitioners took care to show how the resource was used. They took time to address any parent's concerns with respect and explain how they coached children in technique.

In common with other nurseries I have encountered who include woodwork experiences, no child at the woodwork table in Grandpont had ever had more than an ordinary scrape or very minor graze.

It is very good news that best early years practice has reconnected with the power of outdoor learning for young children. Outdoor movements, including Forest School developments, focus on a robust approach to safety and hygiene, which leaves children with plenty of scope to use tools, including knives and to learn how to be safe around fire. Nurseries themselves, as well as organisations like Sightlines Initiative, focus on good communication with children's parents, with explanations, plenty of information and often an opportunity to join a woodland visit to see for themselves.

LOOKING CLOSELY AT FOURS

Young children cannot ask to do something interesting 'again' until they have experienced this opportunity at least once. In Buckingham's Nursery, I watched threes and fours working with large sheets of paper and a generous store of wax crayons. An adult had spread the sheets on a flat surface outdoors and secured them with tyres laid flat. The adult had shown children what was possible, with a brass rubbing technique, but had then sat back to watch them experiment.

The children were very busy making marks, drawing and rubbing hard with their crayons, so that the pattern came through from the texture of the hard surface. The children used a range of correct colour words spontaneously or were able to find me a particular colour, when I asked for 'help' in my search for crayons.

The same resources were fully enjoyed by two-year-olds later in the same afternoon – a useful reminder that appropriate open-ended resources work well across the age range.

young children learn to follow specific directions and judge themselves against the 'right one'. They are less likely to learn a technique that they can then choose to apply in their own projects. If four-year-olds have a history of being overdirected, then you will observe the consequences. Perhaps young girls and boys sit and wait until an adult tells them what to do. The other possibility is that they do their most creative work away from adults and take a splash-and-dash approach to adult-dominated activities. In contrast, children who have experienced a more flexible approach, welcome fresh ideas and then have the confidence to apply them.

Best early years practice is a balancing act of thoughtful adult behaviour as a play partner. It is important that early years practitioners do not feel they must keep away altogether, that any involvement is interference. Children become frustrated if they are left to find out by trial-and-error, when there are more effective ways to use tools or to achieve a particular effect. They welcome friendly guidance with technique in use of tools and materials, and well-judged adult help is also the way to ensure safety, without over-reacting.

Four-year-old creativity in art, craft and activities like gardening can co-exist with safe use of tools and an understanding of hand washing and clearing up afterwards. Children need to be taught useful techniques as appropriate and safety within a practical context. They need access to good quality tools that work. Some gardening or woodwork tools may need to be smaller than the adult version, to fit little hands. However, plastic toy versions are rarely, if ever, a wise choice; they tend to bend and may snap – frequently they do not work either.

Four-year-olds can be very competent with tools, once they have been taught good technique. All the early years provision mentioned in this book had addressed these issues, although each had created a unique indoor and outdoor learning environment. Four-year-olds are able to use proper gardening tools and early years practitioners had coached them in responsible behaviour, without nagging. They had simple ground rules that made sense to the children.

In Grandpont Nursery the children had been taught that tools like a rake were never to be lifted higher than waist height. This ground rule made sense to threes and fours, as they understood that, lifted or swung higher, a rake or similar tool could easily hit someone in the face. They had generalised this rule easily onto how to handle their hockey sticks for their lively outdoor games.

In Grandpont Nursery, New River Green and other settings, I have observed as keen children have learned to use hammers, pliers, a hand drill, saws, nails and sandpaper. I have watched as young children have been shown carefully how to start with soft wood before progressing to the harder pieces. Handy techniques have been shared, such as holding a nail with pliers and then hammering it. Then I have

seen how fours, even some older threes, apply their learning without needing further support.

Flights of imagination

Four-year-olds often show immense creativity through rich pretend play. Using minimal props, four-year-olds explore many different play themes. A regular friendship group will return to the same theme day after day, developing their pirates or dragon story each time. Observant practitioners can offer ideas and some themes, chosen by children, may turn into a semi-permanent role play area.

Four-year-olds show thinking and planning, language skills and recall as they direct play themes themselves, decide on characters, negotiate the 'scripts' and plan out the action to a certain extent. As Vivian Gussin Paley (2004) has shown, feelings can run high when concerns from outside the setting are imported into play by young children. Children may work through a wide range of experiences in play and the task of early years practitioners is to create a positive emotional environment in which this exploration is safe.

Four-year-olds, even those without siblings at home, are often caring towards the younger children, and sometimes welcome them into their play. Not surprisingly, fours become irritated with younger children, siblings or not, if adults allow

LOOKING CLOSELY AT FOURS

Four-year-olds can show creative problem solving, experimentation and working together. During my visit to Grandpont Nursery School a small group of children had designed and built a channel to bring water over some distance from the outdoor tap to their sand pit. Lengths of firm plastic guttering had been supported by milk crates along its length and the system was working well. The head explained to me that the children had worked out their plan and put it into action entirely without adult help. The children had easy access to a wide range of resources to choose and transport to the location of child-initiated enterprises.

The head also explained how they had discussed safety issues with all the children earlier in the year, for instance about a height limit to construction with milk crates. The children had listened to adult explanations that "we don't climb on the crates if they are more than two high, because it's very wobbly, like this...". The head had heard children discuss the height limit and decide on options such as "if we want to climb on them, we'll make it long and not high".

a situation in which the older children rarely get any peace. But the times when social games become squabbling should not detract from the social and communicative skills that four-year-olds show at other times. It is also worth looking out for the sensitive way in which some fours welcome younger children into their pretend play. The advantage for the fours is that threes, and twos as well, are delighted to be playing with the 'big' girls and boys and accept the most mundane of roles.

When they have the opportunity, for instance in provision with babies and toddlers, fours are often keen to be part of the caring routines. Some four-year-olds use their pretend play to explore the practical ideas of baby care and what it means to be much younger. But their understanding is most effectively supported by first-hand experiences with real babies and toddlers. Of course, fours are not left in charge of babies, but they can be competent and enthusiastic assistants to the key person in provision, as well as with their childminder or parent at home. Such experiences, much like riding on a real bus or train, provide the direct knowledge that fours often choose to recycle back into their play.

Over a period of many years, children's creativity in pretend play was limited in many settings by the assumption that any theme with pretend weapons or rumbustious play must be aggressive. Of course, adults are responsible for stepping in to stop genuine physical or emotional hurt between children. Yet this over-concern led to bans in some settings of a wide range of important pretend themes including superheroes, monsters and mythic struggles between goodies and baddies.

LOOKING CLOSELY AT FOURS

At New River Green, several three- and four-year-olds were busy at the woodwork table on the covered veranda. Jamilla and Gaby (two practitioners) sat as part of the group, offering advice when appropriate or requested. Jamilla commented on the wood a child had chosen from the store, saying: "That one's too thick. It will take a very long time to saw". However, this boy decided he wanted to go ahead and the adult supported him. Once he had sawn his wood, he wanted to put it on the 'work in progress' shelf, with his name card, and come back later.

Good technique for sawing is not only more effective, it is also safer. Children heard practical suggestions such as "you need to put the saw in the groove you've made", "it's good to look at what you're doing" and "that's it. Up and down strokes". Sometimes Jamilla or Gaby helped a child to line up the saw. They also ensured that the wood was firmly clamped to the table edge, showing the children what they were doing and why.

The children could paint their wood and nail on other shapes, as they wished. Gaby showed a child how the nail had come through the other side of the two pieces of wood that she had fixed together. The end of the nail now stuck out and the child turned her wood over and hammered the end of the nail over, so it was now flat against her wood.

Three and four-year-olds showed impressive concentration. It takes time to saw through a piece of wood, even the relatively small sections on which they worked – about a centimetre thick and about 15 centimetres wide. But the children focused, even at the tough stage of getting the first sawing groove established. Other children watched, chatted and waited their turn very patiently.

LOOKING CLOSELY AT FOURS

In Mary Paterson Nursery School, three boys (a mix of threes and fours) were very busy in the large outdoor sandpit. They had built a structure of three milk crates on top of each other. A wooden plank was resting against the top, forming a slope up to the structure. They were filling the crates structure up with sand. They occasionally placed one or two big trucks on top. One of the boys balanced on top of the wooden plank before getting off. The boys were able to get other items they needed from the wheeled trolley at the side of the sandpit, which was full of equipment.

Their play flowed between a game about 'Come on, to the rescue' and then moved into a theme around transporting: "The rubbish has to go to the rubbish place". They were filling up the truck parked below the structure with rubbish (sand). They asked me to taste 'some rubbish' on a big ladle and then on a spade. One boy explained that it is "tasty rubbish" and "you should taste it". But they were clear that some of this pretend rubbish is 'yukky'. They were busy distinguishing between 'yummy' or 'yucky' rubbish. They wanted me to 'taste' samples, making the appropriate face each time.

Another boy had joined and was manipulating a long-handled spade to move the rubbish. Then the scenario changed and the sand became 'treasure'. The boys reorganised the crates and sand to make a pirate ship with four spades stuck in it at deliberate angles. The boys' pretend scenario moved seamlessly into dealing with 'baddies'.

WHAT ARE CHILDREN LEARNING?

When you observe four-year-olds' spontaneous pretend play, you see yet again how different areas of their learning weave together within a thoroughly enjoyable experience.

Children use their powers of language and social skills to direct their play and organise each other in physical or imaginative activities. Their language serves a real social purpose in guiding their games and enjoyable interaction. Four-year-olds can be sufficiently confident that they play with words and apply their skills within tuneful exchanges.

Children, who have enjoyed plenty of time to play and explore their own flights of fantasy, can be very creative in using their language to imagine, to create a narrative or work on a pretend play scenario with their friends. Sometimes, a small group is busy retelling and reworking a familiar story from a book, or weaving together several chosen themes.

Fours' physical skills are often central to their competence in building their dens, pirate ships, raised walkways and any other structure that their chosen play theme needs.

LOOKING CLOSELY AT FOURS

In New River Green I watched a half-hour long pretend play sequence in the block area organised by good friends, Rosie (3 years) and Ben (4 years). These two young children moved seamlessly from one theme to another.

At one point, Ben said: "There's a dragon. Quick! Get our swords". Both children picked up short wooden planks, that they held before them like weapons. Rosie said: "We're going to get their fire out" and she and Ben made a sound like rushing water. Rosie explained: "Mine has got fire and water" and Ben said: "Mine has got poo and pee and fire and water".

Ben's mother, who was sitting nearby said mildly: "That sounds a bit smelly" and the practitioner, who was also close, commented with a smile: "But it might sort out the dragon". Rosie and Ben were then discussing sweets. It was unclear whether the dragons were after their pretend sweets or that it was okay for the dragons eat the sweets.

Rosie and Ben now chose to create the scenario of having lunch. The children selected different sized blocks to represent the food they needed and explained that they were laying out the 'food' on the 'tables'. Rosie said: "I've got everything I need" and Ben explained: "We need to cut the food". Rosie giggled and said: "Silly billy – I forgot". Ben took up a plank and said: "It's our measurer".

Rosie looked at the plank and suggested: "This could be our... our... to shoot the very scary dinosaur". Ben appeared to mishear and said with some concern: "You don't shoot fairies". Rosie repeated her idea with: "A very very scary dinosaur". Ben still thought Rosie was talking about shooting fairies and his mother explained: "No, she said 'very very scary – a dinosaur!'".

In this example, the practitioner was able to observe Rosie and Ben's theme about defending their blocks structure against the dragons. The children briefly held pieces as wood as imaginary weapons. But their play remained calm and there was no intervention by the adult.

Penny Holland's (2003) action research was very significant in supporting teams to reconsider what was happening, when two decades of a ban appeared to have achieved little more than restricting rich pretend play themes and teaching children, especially boys, to be secretive about superhero play. I observed in visits to New River Green, and other settings, the effectiveness of lifting this ban for girls, as well as boys.

Further resources

EYFS (2012) Statutory and guidance materials

The Department for Education website is a good one-stop shop for EYFS materials. See: www.education.gov.uk/ schools/teachingandlearning/curriculum/a0068102/ early-years-foundation-stage-eyfs

This site provides access to:

- Department for Education (2012) 'Statutory Framework for the Early Years Foundation Stage: Setting the Standards for Learning, Development and Care for Children from Birth to Five' – this is the statutory guidance, including the safeguarding and welfare requirements, which applies to all early years provision up to and including reception class.

- Early Education (2012) 'Development Matters in the Early Years Foundation Stage (EYFS)' – the non-statutory guidance explaining the four main themes of the EYFS and providing some developmental steps along the way towards the early learning goals.

Books and websites

- Arnold C. (2003) *Observing Harry: Child Development and Learning 0-5*, Open University Press.

- Bilton H. (ed) (2005) *Learning Outdoors: Improving the Quality of Young Children's Play Outdoors*, David Fulton.

- Blythe S. G. (2004) *The Well Balanced Child: Movement and Early Learning*, Hawthorn Press.

- Blythe S. G. (2008) *What Babies and Children Really Need: how Mothers and Fathers Can Nurture Children's Growth for Health and Well Being*, Hawthorn Press.

- British Heart Foundation National Centre (2011) *UK Physical Activity Guidelines for Early Years (Walkers)* www.bhfactive.org. uk/homepage-resources-and-publications-item/280/index.html

- Bromley H. (2006) *Making my own mark: play and writing*, Early Education.

- Campbell R. (1999) *Literacy from Home to School: Reading with Alice*, Trentham Books.

- Caddell D. (1998) *Numeracy Counts*, Scottish Consultative Council on the Curriculum.

- Chilvers D. (2006) *Young Children Talking: the Art of Conversation and Why Children Need to Chatter*, Early Education.

- Community Playthings (2005) *The value of block play*; (2008) *I made a unicorn Children come first*; (2010) *Enabling play: planning environments* (www.communityplaythings.co.uk).

- Cousins J. (2003) 'Listening to four-year-olds: how they can help us plan their education and care', National Children's Bureau.

- Department for Children, Education, Lifelong Learning and Skills (2008) 'Language, Literacy and Communication Skills: 3-7 Foundation Phase', Welsh Assembly Government (http://www.swanseagfl.gov.uk/learn_agenda/ wag_resources/langlitcome.pdf).

- Donaldson M. (1978) *Children's minds*, Fontana.

- Dowling M. (2005) *Supporting young children's sustained shared thinking: an exploration*, Early Education.

- Duckett, R. and Drummond, M.J. (2010) *Adventuring in early childhood education*, Sightlines Initiative (http://www.sightlines-initiative.com/).

- Early Education 'Learning Together' (www.early-education.org.uk).

- EPPE: The Effective Provision of Pre-School Education project (a wide range of papers on www.ioe.ac.uk/schools/ ecpe/eppe).

- Evans B. (2002) *You Can't Come to my Birthday Party: Conflict Resolution with Young Children*, High/Scope Educational Research Foundation.

- Fajerman L.; Jarrett M. and Sutton F. (2000) *Children as partners in planning: a training resource to support consultation with children*, Save the Children.

- Featherstone S. (ed) (2006) *L is for Sheep: getting ready for phonics*, Featherstone Education.

- Featherstone, S. (ed) (2008) *Again, Again: Understanding Schemas in Young Children*, A&C Black.

- Healy J. (2004) *Your Child's Growing Mind: brain development and learning from birth to adolescence*, Broadway.

- Holland P. (2003) *We don't play with guns here: war, weapon and superhero play in the early years*, Open University Press.

- Hughes M. (1986) *Children and number: difficulties in learning mathematics*, Blackwell.

- Hughes A. and Ellis S. (1998) 'Writing it Right? Children Writing 3-8', Scottish Consultative Council.

- Jabadao, undated, *Developmental Movement Play*, Jabadao (www.jabadao.org/?p=developmental.movement.play).

- Jones M. and Belsten J. (2011) *Let's Get Talking: Exciting Ways to Help Children with Speech and Language Difficulties*, Lawrence Educational.

- Lewisham Early Years Advice and Resource Network (2002) *A Place to Learn: Developing a Stimulating Environment*, LEARN.

- Lindon J. (2012 revised edition) *Parents as Partners: Positive Relationships in the Early Years*, Practical Pre-School Books.

- Lindon J. (2013 revised edition) *The Key Person Approach: Positive Relationships in the Early Years,* Practical Pre-School Books.

- Lindon J. (2013 revised edition) *Child-initiated Learning: Positive Relationships in the Early Years*, Practical Pre-School Books.

- Lindon J. (2013 revised edition) *Supporting Children's Social Development: Positive Relationships in the Early Years*, Practical Pre-School Books.

- Lindon J. (2012 revised edition) *Planning for Effective Early Learning*, Practical Pre-School Books.

- Lindon J. (2011) *'Too Safe for Their Own Good? Helping Children Learn about Risk and Life Skills'*, National Children's Bureau.

- Lindon J. (2012) *Planning for the Early Years: The local community*, Practical Pre-School Books.

- Lindon J. (2012a) *Planning for the Early Years: The local community*, Practical Pre-School Books.

- Lindon J. (2012) *Safeguarding and Child Protection 0-8 years*, Hodder Education.

- Lindon J. (2012) *Equality and Inclusion in Early Childhood*, Hodder Education.

- Lindon J. (2012) *Understanding Children's Behaviour: Play, Development and Learning*, Hodder Education.

- Locke A. and Ginsborg J. (2003) 'Spoken language in the early years: the cognitive and linguistic development of three-to five-year-old children from socio-economically deprived backgrounds' *Educational and Child Psychology,* Volume 20.

- Marsden L. and Woodbridge J. (2005) *Looking closely at learning and teaching… a journey of development*, Early Excellence.

- Miller J. (2003) *Never too young: how young children can take responsibility and make decisions – a handbook for early years workers*, Save the Children.

- Moylett H. and Stewart N. (2012) *Understanding the Revised Early Years Foundation Stage*, Early Education.

- Munn P. (1997) 'What do children know about reading before they go to school?' in Owen P. and Pumfrey P. (eds) *Emergent and developing reading: messages for teachers*, Falmer Press.

- Munn P. (1997) 'Children's beliefs about counting' in Thompson I, (ed) *Teaching and learning early number*, Open University Press.

- Nutbrown C. Hannon P. and Morgan A. (2005) *Early literacy work with families: policy, practice and research*, Sage.

- Paley V. G. (2004) *A child's work: the importance of fantasy play*, University of Chicago Press.

- Palmer S. and Bayley R. (2004) *Foundations of Literacy: A Balanced Approach to Language, Listening and Literacy Skills in the Early Years*, Network Educational Press.

- Sightlines Initiative *Rising Sun Woodland Pre-school Project* (www.sightlines-initiative.com).

- Siraj-Blatchford J. and Morgan A. (2009) *Using ICT in the Early Years*, Practical Pre-School Books.

- Siren Films *Firm Foundations for Early Literacy, Falling Out* and the *Outdoors* series of DVDs (www.sirenfilms.co.uk).

- Stevens J. (2012) *Planning for the Early Years: Storytelling and storymaking*, Practical Pre-School Books.

- Thornton L. and Brunton P. (2007) *Bringing the Reggio approach to your early years practice*, David Fulton.

- Tizard B. and Hughes M. (2002) *Young children learning*, Blackwell.

- White J. (2007) *Playing and Learning Outdoors – Making Provision for High Quality Experiences in the Outdoor Environment*, Routledge.

Acknowledgements

I have learned a very great deal over the years from time spent with children, practitioners, parents, early years advisors and college tutors.

I would especially like to thank the following settings for making me welcome in visits from which I gained ideas and the examples used in this book: Buckingham's Nursery School (Leek); Burnwood Nursery School (Staffordshire); Grandpont Nursery School (Oxford); Mary Paterson Nursery School (Queens Park); New River Green Early Years Centre and Family Project (Islington); Poplar Play Centre (Poplar); Saplings Nursery (Shortlands); St Peter's Eaton Square CE Primary School Nursery Class (Pimlico); St Mark's Square Nursery School (Camden); Start Point Sholing (Southampton); The Grove Nursery School (Camberwell); Windham Nursery School (Sheen). Thank you also to Louise Davies of Town and Country Kiddies (Louth) for her shared example.

I much appreciate what I have learned from working with Early Excellence, Sightlines Initiative, Siren Films and the What Matters To Children team. My thanks also to Penny Munn and Penny Tassoni, who have been generous in sharing ideas, and Jan Dubiel for his thoughtful approach to outcomes and creativity.

I have changed the names of any children and adults in examples observed in actual settings. Drew and Tanith are my own (now adult) son and daughter and they have given permission for me to quote from the informal diaries I kept of their first five years.

Thanks go to Crescent II Kindergarten, Mary Paterson Nursery School, Grove House Children's Centre and the Little Rainbow Nursery for permission to use the photos in this book.

What does it mean to be four?

Notes

Notes